★ ★ ★ ★ ★

"Bloggers understand that the substance in the information reformation is key to the future survival and success of our families, nation, and world. This is why I believe that joining the **MuscleHead Revolution** becomes imperative. Arming yourself with a fistful of sensibility is how you prepare to wage the war for truth, justice, and all that is good. So get out of the bunker, stand a post, and advance the lines today—become a **MuscleHead!**"

Hugh Hewitt
Nationally syndicated talk show host
New York Times bestselling author of *If It's Not Close,*
They Can't Cheat and *Blog: Inside the Information Reformation*

★ ★ ★ ★ ★

"Make no Mistake—Many Minutes with McCullough will Morph your Mind into a **MuscleHead!**"

David Wheaton
Author of *University of Destruction*
Radio talk show host

★ ★ ★ ★ ★

"It's time for everyone to join the **MuscleHead Revolution**. Never has reinforcing faith, defending truth, and ensuring our values been so important. And never has there been a more powerful tool in pursuit of these goals."

Ben Shapiro
Syndicated columnist
Bestselling author of *Brainwashed* and *Porn Generation*

★ ★ ★ ★ ★

"The **MuscleHead Revolution,** with Kevin McCullough at its vanguard, challenges all of us out of our intellectual complacency and calls us to active duty in the great debates of our time. We cannot sit on the sidelines, content to grow fat between the ears while our opponents claim the contest by default. Kevin reminds us that we must exercise our wit and rely on our faith to return to America its sense of mission and its central purpose of spreading freedom and liberty at home and abroad. The **MuscleHead Revolution** delivers us from decades of moral relativism and defeatism that discounts honor, faith, and freedom."

Edward Morrissey
Captain's Quarters Blog
Conservative Blogger of the Year 2004

★ ★ ★ ★ ★

"Conservative Republicans ostensibly control the White House and Congress, but all too often it seems as if liberal Democrats are still running the show in Washington. The GOP needs an immersion course in **MuscleHead** guerilla politics to learn how to confront their opponents head on and use the ammunition at their disposal."

Carl Limbacher
"Inside Cover" editor, NewsMax.com

MUSCLEHEAD
REVOLUTION

Nancy,
Keep fighting the
fight!
GOOD
Ps. 115:3

Kevin
McCullough

HARVEST HOUSE PUBLISHERS

EUGENE, OREGON

Cover by Left Cost Design, Portland, Oregon

Cover photo © Deborah Davis/Workbook.com

MUSCLEHEAD REVOLUTION
Copyright © 2006 by Kevin McCullough
Published by Harvest House Publishers
Eugene, Oregon 97402
www.harvesthousepublishers.com

McCullough, Kevin, 1970—MuscleHead revolution / Kevin McCullough.
   p. cm.
  ISBN-13: 978-0-7369-1730-8 (pbk.)
  ISBN-10: 0-7369-1730-6
1. Christianity and politics—United States. 2. Liberalism—Religious aspects—Christianity. 3. Conservatism—Religious Aspects—Christianity. 4. Liberalism—United States. 5. Conservatism—United States. 6. Christianity and culture—United States. I. Title.
  BR517.M375 2006
  320.520973—dc22   200609773

Printed in the United States of America

06 07 08 09 10 11 12 13 14 / RDC-KB / 10 9 8 7 6 5 4 3 2 1

In memory of Sharon Shetter McCullough,
who always took the time to teach me what was right...
and who did her best to live it before me.

Contents

The New Media and the MuscleHeads

Foreword by Hugh Hewitt

Kevin McCullough is a young man with experiences the envy of those far older.

He's a veteran of old media who is using his talent on radio to forge a new coalition that lives both on AM and FM as well as the Web. McCullough has been on the air for more than two decades, and not in out-of-the-way markets, but in major markets such as New York and Chicago. His weekly audience is larger than 95 percent of the radio hosts on the air today.

But he's not content to just work over the airwaves and prosper as his audience grows. That would be too easy, and it would also be a waste of his many gifts. Which is why Kevin embraced the new media, blogging—he's been very prolific at it.

And as you will see in *MuscleHead Revolution*, Kevin McCullough is on a mission.

That mission is rooted in his deep Christian faith and his mature patriotism. It is informed by his intellect, disciplined by his careful theology, and powered by his passion for truth.

It also helps a lot that he's a funny guy.

Kevin understands that ultimately, the gospel is best spread by men and women who have taken the time to learn how to articulate it clearly, and that the political freedoms that allow for the transmission of the faith are best defended by men and women who know how to work smart and not just hard. And by folks who are, above all, winsome.

So Kevin spends his time talking and writing as an example to those who share his concern for moral values and common sense. As you read through this book, you will find yourself—again and again—saying, "Of course!" That's what Kevin is hoping for, and that's what I am certain you will find.

Eternal truth doesn't change, but the contexts in which it must be defended do. The arguments of the mid-twentieth century and the methods of delivering those arguments don't resonate with the adults of the early twenty-first century, and especially not with the young adults of today.

But the current generations of people don't need the truth any less. They just need new messengers with new means of delivery.

Or in the case of Kevin, many means.

Kevin has succeeded on air and in print because he listens far more than he lectures; he engages far more often than he advises; and he persuades rather than pontificates at every turn.

The Musclehead Revolution had a beachhead in Chicago, and then it moved to New York City. From its base in New York it has moved online, and with the publication of this book, it is now available through bookstores everywhere.

Do yourself a favor and read this book closely, and with a marker in hand. Then pass the annotated book along to a friend or family member. Or better yet, order a few additional copies to give to those close to you. In the gift greeting, include Kevin's Web site address http://muscleheadrevolution.com as well as the hours (adjusted for time zone!) when your friend or relative can listen to Kevin online.

Kevin McCullough is more than a broadcaster, syndicated columnist, and an author...he's an example of how to fight the good fight, and how to do it well.

Pass the word along.

Hugh Hewitt
Nationally syndicated talk show host
New York Times best-selling author of *Blog: Inside the Information Reformation*

A Wake-up Call

On November 2, 2004, more voters than ever before in the history of elections in the United States of America voiced their opinions in polling places across the country.

There was much unknown about how the day would turn out.

And while the focal point was the presidential election, there were many other issues on the table—issues that stirred this record-breaking voter turnout. For starters, the candidates in the race for president had battled to a statistical dead heat, and prognosticators were looking intensely at turnout county by county in the magical "swing states." Voters everywhere poured out of bed before sunrise and stood in long lines at elementary school cafeterias or church basements, all in an effort to lend their vote to the man they hoped would be president of the United States for the next four years.

It had been a campaign unlike any previous. Never had so much money been spent by both parties. Never had so much money glutted the system outside of the parties. The fate of one of the candidates hung on forged memos that were the basis for a knowingly false report perpetrated by a major news organization.

The fate of the other candidate had been thoroughly decimated by a campaign commercial that cost only $200,000 to put on the air. That a $200,000 commercial had so much power was amazing because the total amount spent by both campaigns went into the hundreds of millions of dollars.

Midway through election day, exit polls began to be reported. These polls made it appear as though one party and its candidate were clearly winning. Yet as was true about many other issues related to the elections of 2004, the manipulation of appearances had been masterful. That manipulation succeeded for a few hours and was just one aspect of a larger strategy to influence the election's outcome.

What seemed odd at the time was that the exit polls were so one-sided, even though the race itself had been locked in a dead heat for weeks. Things weren't adding up. And eventually the truth came out.

I remember the frustration that I felt as I heard that the exit polls were not serving as accurate predictors of the election's outcome. I remember noticing that the numbers the exit polls showed were not even representative of the actual demographics in some areas. I remember how I rolled up my sleeves and started wading through online news sites and blogs to see if others were making the same observations. I remember how thankful I was to see that I wasn't alone, and better yet, that some sources were noting that the exit polls were weighing the turnout samples in a biased manner and were apparently getting their results from largely Democratic counties and polling centers.

As these revelations became known, I went on the air and encouraged my listeners to not pay any attention to what they may or may not have heard about the exit poll numbers. In the New York City area the polls were scheduled to remain open for another six hours, and I said, "Just make sure you fulfill your civic duty and get out there before they close."

As the night dragged on and the exit polling data continued to be exposed for the fraud that it had been designed to be, it became obvious to America that real change had occurred in people's minds and hearts since the election of 2000. Here in 2004, it would not come down to Florida, hanging chads, or the Supreme Court. Instead, the winner in 2000 had increased his total votes in 2004 by an amazing four to five percent nationally, in nearly every county.

Obviously he didn't win every county. But all across America, four more people out of every 100 said, "We need a strong leader in these changing times" and cast their vote to re-elect George W. Bush.

Now before I go any further, let me tell you this book isn't about Republicans and Democrats. It's not about one's party affiliation. It's about us and America—what's best for us as a nation. And much of what happened in the 2004 election relates to the MuscleHead Revolution, which I'll explain in a moment.

What led to this significant change in voter sentiment from 2000 to 2004? According to postelection surveys, the number-one motivating factor above all the others was moral values. In retrospect, even the party that did not win affirmed this fact on all the Sunday shows and political pundit programs.

Americans who were concerned about moral values had come out in the largest total numbers in the history of the nation (in terms of percentage of eligible voters)—the highest in four election cycles. In doing so they exercised what I call on my radio show "the McCullough Muscle"—the brain. The moral values their parents had instilled in them since childhood had come under attack. It had happened on their watch, and in response, they did the only commonsense thing to do: fight back. To these voters, moral values are an extension of who they are and what they believe.

Especially important is that surveys revealed these voters were both religious and nonreligious. Common sense was telling them that sliding down the slope of moral excess was not what was best for America. And contrary to what some might think, these voters aren't just now embracing moral values. They've held to them all along. The 2004 election simply served as the catalyst that made them realize they needed to speak up. They had been awakened!

What stirred some of this impassioned response at the polls?

In 11 states, one of the fiercest battles ever waged was on the ballot. Should marriage be redefined to include any type of arrangement society could come up with? By margins—ranging from 80 percent in Mississippi to nearly 60 percent in the liberal bastion of Oregon—voters loudly proclaimed, "No!"

And there were other battles being waged. In multiple ways, a vote in the 2004 election was a vote to preserve America's moral fiber or further undermine it. That's why so many saw the election in 2004 as the most important presidential vote of their lifetime. Again, this did not happen because a "new majority" of Americans were persuaded to think this way. Rather these people, who believed in common sense, already existed, and they did so in large numbers.

Sometimes they don't always know quite why they believe something is wrong or right. But their instincts are strong, and they are familiar with common sense. It is these commonsense thinkers—that is, *MuscleHeads*—who stood up on election day 2004 and said, "Enough is enough."

Who are these MuscleHeads?

MuscleHeads are deeply concerned about facts, integrity, and honor. Some of them are Democrats, some are Republicans. Neither makes you a MuscleHead, and neither excludes you from being one.

MuscleHeads regret seeing the land most full of freedom and the possibility for good be constantly, ripped to shreds by the media, torn down by enemies from abroad, and stabbed in the back by those from within who do not appreciate or champion the higher ideals of freedom, honor, integrity, and virtue.

MuscleHeads might go to church. They might be people of faith. They may even read the Bible from time to time. But the key common denominators shared by all MuscleHeads are that they care about their families, their children, their communities, and the future.

Election day 2004 was an opportunity for MuscleHeads to vent their frustration, and vent they did.

Maybe you have wanted to help regain some of what our country has lost, and just haven't been sure how to do that. That's what this book is all about.

Every single day we are blasted with thousands of messages from the media, political leaders, persons of influence, and sometimes even clergy members, and at times they send messages that are not good for us. How can we determine which messages are filled with common sense and are helpful? And which ones are not and are destructive? Most importantly, how can we tell when we are being told the truth or being sold a truckload of fertilizer?

The copy of MuscleHead Revolution that you now hold in your hand will arm you with the key principles of commonsense thinking. They have been kept short and memorable, and they are designed to be digested quickly, and practiced often. They will become your armor in the battles ahead. They will equip you to not only defend yourself when the enemy attacks, but also to go on the offense with confidence and fight for all that is good.

And a warning here: You'll find the principles in MuscleHead Revolution very relevant to everyday life. This is no accident. You'll become more empowered as these principles take root in your life and grow. That's why you will want to read this book over and over. So go ahead and feel free to mark up the pages and underline the key points. Do whatever it takes to make these principles your own.

That will make them come to life for you and enable you to take the action you've always wanted to take.

We in the MuscleHead Revolution have committed ourselves to taking steps forward. We will use the faculties we have to outthink our enemies both foreign and domestic. We will fight with all that's within us. But there is more.

> We will be winsome.
>
> We will be charming.
>
> We will be intelligent.
>
> We will be aggressive.
>
> We will take the fight anywhere needed.
>
> We will never surrender.

After all, the problems that stirred the hearts of those who voted on November 2, 2004 have not been solved. There is still a very serious and appalling lack of commonsense thinking all around us. It's up to us to take a stand and fight so that our children are not left to fight these battles too.

Well, that's what *MuscleHead Revolution* is all about. We MuscleHeads did not choose this war. But we must, and I believe we will, win it.

So…are you ready to join the MuscleHead Revolution?

1
The Diabolical Dagger Society

K evin, I ran across your show the other day and I was glued to the seat. Even after I got home from the store and the ice cream was melting in my car, I could not stop listening until the end of the segment because of what you were discussing."

That's what the caller—we'll call her Jane—said as we talked about one of the most controversial issues to capture the attention of our nation, the battle over Terri Schiavo.

"What I don't understand," Jane continued, "is that it seems so illogical to believe what the mainstream press is feeding us by way of actual facts in the case. If I had not heard the voice of the doctor who actually examined Terri on your show just moments ago, I wouldn't be able to believe it for myself."

Jane concluded, "It is as though the mainstream media are asking me to believe them...when my mind and heart both know that to do so makes absolutely no sense."

I could feel the angst in Jane's words. I felt the emotion that she exuded as the realization was creeping over her. She had been betrayed by the media coverage she had seen on the Schiavo case. She had not been told of the finer nuances that brought this crisis into sharper focus. But when those nuances were made a part of the public discourse, her feelings and beliefs about the case began to shift. And, according to Jane, they shifted dramatically.

I just wish that Jane's experience was not so common. I long for the day when people like Jane can be empowered by access to full and honest information. However, until that day, MuscleHeads must stay on the offense, knowing that the mainstream media rarely tell the full story.

While Jane is not alone, the overwhelming supposed "consensus" portrayed by the national media can cause her to feel isolated and cut off. Millions of people each day open a newspaper or turn on the nightly news only to be told, "This is what you should believe." And without due diligence on the part of the individual, they are none the wiser.

Identifying the Opponents

While the media is the mouthpiece for much of the one-sided stream of propaganda that is fed to society every day, "McCullough MuscleHeads" are learning that the media is by no means alone in the effort. There are other culprits involved behind the scenes. And on my broadcast, we have come up with a name for those whose collective influence works to undermine what we believe is good in our life and society. We have identified those who either manipulate the truth, don't tell the whole story, or challenge the values we hold dear, and we will not let them escape unscathed.

We call them the Diabolical Dagger Society, or DDS for short.

We call them *diabolical* because they oppose what we believe to be good and right. Whether they are aware of the diabolical nature of their efforts matters not. Their intent is to undermine the traditional idea of truth, justice, and what is good and right.

They use *daggers* in the form of rhetoric and nonsensical logic. Sometimes they use other weapons at their disposal. A judge may slant the interpretation of a law so as to "find a right" that is never spelled out in even the most basic reading of a piece of legislation. Or a screenwriter might mock sexual purity through seemingly innocuous jokes.

What's scary about daggers is that they are a weapon used at close range. In order to use one in a lethal way, the attacker must be close enough to their intended target to get a blade (which is much smaller than a sword) near enough to the victim's heart or a vital organ before betraying the harmful intent. This symbolism is not lost on true MuscleHeads. We know it well. We regularly have courts tell us that the right to life is nothing compared to the right to privacy. We have academic institutions tell us that they know better how to teach values to our children than we parents do. Then when they teach our children, we discover that they in fact share nothing of our values whatsoever. Getting close enough to their intended target to wound them is key to the success of the DDS.

And we label it a *society* for one simple reason. It is the liberal elites in this country who believe they know better than everyone else. It is from the halls of liberal senators, black-robed justices, tenured professors, and top editorial boardrooms that the society seeks to impose its morally bankrupt, indecent, and destructive influence upon the larger civilization that does not want it and believes strongly that they do not need it.

Obviously not every academic, judge, media person, or politician is a member of the DDS. But enough are, such that their influence on society is significant and pervasive.

Examining the Tactics

Through the activist reassignment of legislative duties pushed ahead by the "bullies in black robes" chapter of the DDS, the most radical and liberal elements in American culture have been able to accomplish from the bench what "we the people" would never have allowed them to accomplish right in front of us. Through the university campus, the ivory tower chapter of the DDS seeks to undo in one semester what parents have tried to impart for 18 years. And through the lens of Hollywood, the media element of the DDS imposes upon pop culture the worldview that the elites in movie and television production studios wish us to adopt. This three-prong attack is not always able to be spotted easily. So before we look at the ways we can win the MuscleHead Revolution, and win we will, we need to see up close the dangers we are all currently exposed to.

There are likely some who doubt whether victory is possible. After all, according to the biblical text, our world will continue to decline until the Messiah returns. Yet that same text promises a bright hope of what that return ultimately means—complete victory over sin and death for those who know Him. This means that as these battles rage on, we do not fight aimlessly. We do not fight without a sense of purpose. Our role is to remain faithful and to slow the onslaught of everything and everyone that seeks to destroy what is true, just, and good. Standing on our Rock of Ages, and relying upon the weapons of truth that never fades and faith that does not fail, we can fight with certainty regarding the final outcome of human history.

The rest of this chapter may not be easy to consume. It may make you squirm. But we are not ready to win the war until we can readily identify the tactics our opponents utilize. So let's look at some examples of how the DDS has waged its battle campaigns.

Redefining Marriage

One of the more obvious places in American culture where the DDS is wreaking havoc is in the American understanding of the institution of marriage. And the perspectives they could not "sell" to the American people outright are frequently advanced through trickery.

In the fall of 2003, the U.S. Supreme Court ruled, in the now infamous case *Lawrence v. Texas*, that the state of Texas was unconstitutional in its enforcement of anti-sodomy statutes. The court defended its ruling by claiming "equal protection" violation under the state statute that penalized sodomy between homosexual men yet did not offer a similar penalty against married couples who engaged in the same activity.

When the decision was handed down, reaction was immediate. Gay rights groups all across the country saw this as a doorway of opportunity to push a more aggressive agenda in moving the nation toward redefining marriage.

MuscleHeads saw it similarly. Senator Rick Santorum, among others, was quick to identify publicly that future courts would no doubt see the equal access clause in the high court's ruling as precedent-setting. Santorum argued that the high court's decision could lead other courts to resort to the "equal protection" argument for redefining marriage.

Sure enough, before the year ended, the Massachusetts State Supreme Court, in a 4–3 ruling, used that very thinking to justify ordering that state's legislature to officially redefine marriage. The legislature mulled multiple options, but ultimately caved in to the court's instruction.

Within weeks, cases in California, Oregon, Texas, Michigan, and New York were winging their way through their individual judicial systems. In addition, rogue mayors in San Francisco, California and New Paltz, New York went so far as to issue marriage licenses to same-sex couples in open violation of state laws. And even though the licenses were deemed illegitimate on a temporary basis, the issue was front and center. In more than one case, the attention was such that the issue at hand avoided lengthy lower court scrutiny and gained direct admittance to state appellate or supreme courts. As of the writing of this chapter, some of these cases are still being decided.

Sexualizing Our Children

Another area in which the DDS has advanced its attacks on common sense is in relation to the welfare of our children.

I have long held to a socialization theory that goes something like this: The ultimate goal of today's sexual revolution is to achieve the ancient Roman and Greek sexual standard of making sexual playthings of children. There are many ways in which this mindset is taking root in America, and it is deeply distressing to those of us who love our kids and want to leave behind a safer place than we inherited.

It should not be surprising to anyone that as immorality runs rampant and reaches new lows in our country our children have been increasingly at risk. Some 40 years after the start of the sexual revolution, during which "free love" and "if it feels good, do it" were the mantras of the time, we now see an escalating number of nightly news stories of pedophiles kidnapping, molesting, and murdering children. For months we saw nightly news updates about a pop star who allegedly allowed underage children to sleep in his bed after exposing them to porn.

The increasingly frequent issuance of an "Amber Alert" somewhere in America has become so routine that people practically yawn their way through them as they hurry onward in their busy lives.

What are among the ways our children have been put more at risk in our society?

The simple answer is, "All things dangerous to them."

Television now delivers thousands of viewing options per day, as opposed to the mere three network channels of two generations ago. Video rental stores are located in every community, almost always with a large selection of DVDs that contain an abundance of sexually explicit material. High-speed Internet now gives the average home access to more than 200 million pornography sites.

We must keep in mind that at the core of the cultural debate and how it affects our children is the fact that there are people who are leading the charge of approving all of this material.

And that brings us back to members of the Diabolical Dagger Society.

Many media producers—be they television, Internet, film, or print—are certainly on the front lines of this problem. They rake in millions, live in gated communities, and are relatively cut off from how you and I and other concerned members of the MuscleHead Revolution go through life.

In addition, there are specific individuals who justify and promote a core belief system, a philosophical "brand" that justifies these worst of all human instincts. One of the more notable champions of the sexualizing of children has argued for this on paper.

Judith Levine is a writer and an academic. Her book was released by the University of Minnesota Press in 2003. In it she makes striking statements about the state of children today in relationship to sex, and she draws a number of assumptions about the world we live in now. She argues that it is too prudish. She believes that children without sexual knowledge are being wronged in the manner in which they are being taught to think about sex. She also believes that literally unlimited sexual partners for children should be fine as long as they are protected from unwanted sexual activity, and so long as they practice said sex "safely." She believes that sex between consenting children and adults might not be harmful to the children involved.

The book, interestingly enough, is titled *Harmful to Minors: The Perils of Protecting Children from Sex.* As if the idea of "protecting" children somehow damages them?

The book's foreword was penned by Dr. Joycelyn Elders, who became infamous for advocating mandatory condom distribution in public schools as well as taxpayer-funded birth control. She advocated these while serving as the U.S. Surgeon General under President Clinton.

On this point of sexualizing children, then, we see a triple play being executed. Academia is setting the philosophical boundaries. Politicians are setting the public policy mandates. And Hollywood comes behind them to push the envelope of public acceptance.

Promoting the Culture of Death

Yet another arena in which the war on common sense presents a very real danger is in today's "culture of death."

We have reached an unprecedented stage of lack of respect for human life. We have come to a point in time where the taking of innocent human life has broken barriers never before seen.

Taking the Lives of Babies

In 1973 with the advent of *Roe v. Wade,* Norma McCorvey (who was Jane Roe) was persuaded by radical pro-death activists who sought permanent legal protections in the act of killing an innocent unborn child. Twisting logic in ways that defy belief, the activists first conned themselves, then their supporters, followed by McCorvey, and eventually the liberal justices of the U.S. Supreme Court into believing that unborn children were not living human beings. To agree with the pro-death activists requires us to swallow the moral ethics concoction that goes against provable science, heartfelt emotional connection between mother and baby, and most of all, the common sense that comes from experiencing the process of pregnancy.

The culture of death has now tread beyond killing more than 44 million unborn children since *Roe v. Wade* and moved to advance death in additional arenas.

Taking the Lives of the Terminally Ill

For example, the "right to die" movement emerged only a few years after *Roe v. Wade.* An early pioneer of controversial "mercy deaths," Dr. Jack Kervorkian, who became known as Dr. Death, earned his infamy through multiple successful attempts in assisting others in the taking of their own lives. He did this in spite of strict state statutes that explicitly outlawed such physician assistance.

As Dr. Death went through his personal campaign of boldly helping in the taking of these lives, and furthermore documenting them on video, public pressure began to be exerted on both sides of the right-to-die effort. Big-time Hollywood celebrities began to "Back Jack," as one of the campaigns turned the phrase. The main cry of support from these backers was that we should allow those who suffer from terminal illness to "die with dignity." "No one should be made to suffer excruciating pain, especially when terminal illness is predicating the outcome," was the common argument of the day.

Those who opposed the culture of death had a different view. Their arguments stemmed from the ideas that life itself was good and that doing what was necessary to protect it was honorable. The thought that doctors who had taken oaths to protect life were now using medical knowledge to accelerate life's end also greatly bothered them. The slippery slope upon which the culture of death advocates had embarked, they argued, would eventually lead to the killing of the nonterminally ill.

And these opponents were right, as we will now see.

Taking the Lives of the Nonterminally Ill
The Terri Schiavo Case

In early 2005, America watched history unfold in the battle between the cultures of life vs. death. For years a husband intent on ending the life of his wife—with the support of a probate judge—had worked his plan to make a statement in what had widely become known as the most famous right-to-die case ever.

Michael Schiavo had argued successfully before probate judge George Greer that his wife, Terri Schindler Schiavo, would not have wanted to live in what Michael called "a persistent vegetative state."

Michael, Terri's "husband," according to court records, had been intimate with another woman 18 months after Terri's collapse from cardiac arrest in 1990. Michael then went on to father two children by yet a third woman. Even though Michael's extramarital involvement with other women was well documented, he was still allowed to determine Terri's fate.

The doctors who examined Terri on behalf of Michael were noted right-to-die advocates. The attorney who represented Michael and, by proxy, Terri was also a right-to-die advocate.

And the striking difference in this case—in contrast to those Kervorkian had been associated with—was that Terri was not terminally ill. She had suffered brain injury for sure, but so have thousands of other Americans who can no longer speak for themselves. She needed assistance to do a great number of basic things, but so did Christopher Reeve following his paralysis. Terri needed reparative therapy, which the court allowed her husband to deny. She needed antibiotics to fight off urinary tract infections, but the court allowed her husband to say no. And yet after nearly 14 years in that condition, Terri had developed, on her own, a 13-word vocabulary.

Never before in the history of our nation had a husband been allowed to go before a court, request permission to starve his wife to death (especially one who was burdened with special needs), and then been granted that permission. But with Terri Schiavo that line was crossed, and an innocent woman was mercilessly starved as the nation watched. And while good people were paralyzed by the shocking inability of the Congress, a governor, and a president to save this woman's life, the culture-of-death vultures circled and threatened to use those elected officials' intervention against them as a political weapon in the upcoming elections.

It hadn't taken long for us to slip downward from killing unborn children to killing the terminally ill and then to the taking of someone's life because he or she is inconvenient to care for. But what about the forcible taking of someone else's life against the will of those involved?

A disturbing example of this came within the midst of Terri Schiavo's passing.

Abuse and Abortion in Granite City

There is a good chance you have never heard of the Hope Abortion Clinic in Granite City, Illinois. But in the middle of the two weeks during which we were watching Terri Schiavo be killed via starvation on our television screens, an incident occurred there that was even more unbelievable. Jill Stanek, a fellow columnist with *World Net Daily* and the news staff of the *Illinois Leader*, championed the coverage of the Granite City incident. The following is a summary of the story as it unfolded in March 2005.

According to published reports, a 14-year-old girl whom Stanek refers to as "Nicole" had told her parents, just weeks earlier, that she had made a horrible mistake with her boyfriend, "Mark." They had slept together, and she was now pregnant.

Nicole comes from a conservative family. Her parents are Baptists, and they had tried their best to teach Nicole right from wrong. In spite of that upbringing, Nicole, at age 14, found herself in a dangerous and vulnerable position. Nicole's parents assured her that she had made the right decision when she told them she was pregnant, and pledged that they would stand by her through the pregnancy.

According to Stanek's account, Nicole's mom took her to the New Beginnings Pregnancy Care Center in Granite City on March 15. New Beginnings showed Nicole and her mom the baby's heartbeat via an ultrasound. They also were able to determine the child's gender—it was a boy. As Nicole and her mother rode home that afternoon, they discussed the child's name.

Nicole settled on Bradley. She loved that name and commented to her mother how resolved she was to let him live.

Unfortunately Mark's parents were not so resolved.

According to Stanek, Mark's parents insisted that Nicole get an abortion. During one run-in between the two families, Mark whined about how the baby would ruin his plans, his life, and his future. Mark's mother proudly stated that she had aborted some five babies already and wouldn't think twice about aborting one again. Mark's father insisted that Nicole's parents should have no say in the matter—that ultimately, it was Nicole's decision to make. Mark's mother is even quoted as having said, "You probably hate that baby inside you, don't you?"

Nicole was torn. She had seen the ultrasound. But her feelings were still very much blooming for Mark, and she did not wish to displease him or his family.

Only two days after the ultrasound was performed, a shocking series of events unfolded. According to published reports, Mark's mother phoned Nicole's school posing as Nicole's grandmother and getting her relieved of classes for the day. Sometime in the early morning hours before Nicole's mom had returned from her job as a school bus driver and her dad from his overnight job, Mark and his mother picked up

Nicole and took her to the largest abortuary in the Midwest. When Nicole's dad returned from work, he was surprised not to find her at home preparing for the school day. Suspecting the worst, he phoned Nicole's mom, who grabbed a friend and made a beeline for the abortion mill. To get past the outer security checkpoint, Nicole's mother clutched her stomach and told the guards she needed to see a counselor.

Once inside, the mother spotted Nicole's name on the admission list. She had been admitted at 7:45 AM It was then roughly 8:30 AM She was told there was no one who fit Nicole's description admitted to the clinic.

Anticipating that there would eventually be a scene, Nicole's mother turned to her friend and told her to deal with security when they were called. She then began to call for Nicole by name up and down the hallways of the clinic.

Nicole later admitted she heard her mother calling her and requested the staff tending to her to get a message to her mom. The staff left for a few moments, then returned to tell Nicole that her mother had left the premises.

Eventually the police subdued Nicole's mother, cuffed her, and shoved her in the back of a squad car. She pleaded with the police to go in and help her daughter. According to Stanek's account, the mother was told to "see her senator."

Nicole was immediately bumped to the front of the line for procedures that morning. And at 10:35 AM Nicole was released from the clinic through the front door, armed only with a paper bag in case she experienced any vomiting. She had thrown up three times already during her brief recovery period.

During the commotion, Mark and his mother had been allowed to leave the clinic out the back door, and they immediately left for a vacation to Florida.

By contrast, Nicole experienced back pain, tender breasts, and the discharge of blood clots in the aftermath of her procedure. All that was done to Nicole that morning violated her rights as a minor, violated her parents' sovereignty as her guardians, and took the life of a child she had only two days previous decided to name Bradley.

Planning for Victory

As we consider Terri's tragic death and the horror that 14-year-old Nicole had been exposed to (even against the wishes of her parents), one fact is painfully clear: The Diabolical Dagger Society is intent on undermining and destroying not just philosophical institutions and structures, but real human lives. They may in fact be targeting you, your family, your children, or your future. The days of quiet discussion and gracious assumptions that the DDS will play by the rules are over. We are not in a polite boxing match with padded gloves and a referee. We are in a back-alley brawl, and the members of the DDS have their switchblades and broken bottles at the ready. The question now arises: Are *we* ready?

The Diabolical Dagger Society is real, and now the war they have started is raging. In the pages to come we will learn the keys to implementing a victorious battle plan. We will unpack key principles, one by one, that will build the muscle between our ears. We will see that when we equip ourselves with truth and common sense, we can fight back. We will see that when we couple truth with faith, there's nothing stopping us.

And for the record, when I speak of faith in the pages ahead, I will do so from the deepest convictions of my heart. I will reference the God who created us as well as His Son, whom God sent to save us. I will also reference to the truth found in His Word, for He is the origin of truth.

We who consider ourselves MuscleHeads must now arm ourselves so we can enter the fray and, battle by battle, strive toward victory in this war. Or, we should at least die trying.

There really is no alternative. The high price of doing nothing is the loss of our innocence, our honor, and our lives.

2

It's God, Stupid!

Election day November 2004 was as memorable as it was long. The lines at the polling places opened early on the East Coast and did not shut down out west for another 15 hours. As voters decided which presidential candidate they wanted to see entrusted with the care of our nation for the next four years, they did so with a different set of concerns than they had in 1992.

Twelve years previous, the mantra had been "It's the economy, stupid" as the nation swept William Jefferson Clinton into office. But then many became scarred as they watched with shock as marriage was made a mockery of through sexual misconduct in the Oval Office. And the early signs of an Islamic terrorist uprising became evident in a bombing attack on the World Trade Center and another one on the U.S.S. Cole.

We also saw the Clinton economy slide into recession even before he was out of office. We saw his Vice President Al Gore place himself above the rule of law in the raising of campaign funds and utter the phrase "no controlling authority" when asked about it by the press.

When President George W. Bush took office, he inherited a sinking economy and immediately began to address the tax code, lowering taxes across the board for the first time in eight years. He passed an educational reform bill with the help of prominent Democrats. And he made it clearly evident to the nation that he cherished his wife.

Then came the events of September 11 and the subsequent global War on Terror. For many of President's Bush's critics, this was the moment he "grew up." Many of his supporters felt that the character they had seen in him as a candidate now had the opportunity to come to the surface and be seen for what it was. And for many, critic or supporter, the nation began to know more of the deeply important role faith plays in the life of President Bush.

On stem-cell research, partial-birth abortion, and the radical attempts by the courts to redefine marriage, the mainstream of America found in President Bush a man who reflected their moral views. And even in the war against terror, many voters recognized that the terrorists were attacking not just America, but the value system many of us hold to.

If there was a lesson to be learned by politicians from the record turnout of votes that the Republican party garnered in November of 2004 it was this: God is important to the grassroots voter. And even apart from professed belief in God there is still an overwhelming majority of American voters who, to a large extent, do not wish to see culture turn its back on the values that represent them.

For days, weeks, and months after the election liberals were left scratching their heads. "How could America be so conservative?" they asked themselves.

And for liberal elites, the beating was especially hard to take. For months they had crafted the campaign as "the enlightened vs. the ignorant." So it was with genuine earnestness that the liberal elites pondered, "Don't these idiot voters know that this guy is a buffoon?"

The liberal left's contempt for people of faith and their values had so blinded them during the campaign season that they never let themselves believe for a moment that this "faith and values thing" would affect the turnout of the election.

But perhaps you are slightly left of center, or you believe yourself to be progressive, and you still have questions about how the election turned. I'm glad you've read this far. Let's take a look at what happened.

Where the Liberals Went Wrong

One person who was very much shocked by the election outcome in 2004 was Democratic presidential candidate John Kerry. Off the record, there were reports of Kerry becoming furious behind the scenes. Liberal pundits such as Susan Estrich, Bob Beckel, and Alan Colmes sat dumbfounded in front of TV cameras. "Don't tell us we don't believe in moral values," said liberal Democrats. "What about caring for the poor, helping those in need, and working towards peace in the world—aren't these moral values?"

One of the great misnomers in "poli-talk" today is to advocate that only one of the two major parties believes in feeding the hungry and housing the homeless. Liberals want us all to believe that they are the only party that does anything about such needs, but that's just not true.

Both conservatives and liberals desire to "help the poor, feed the hungry, and bring about peace on earth." The difference between the two groups is how these things should be done. We'll delve more into that later, but suffice it to say for now that liberals have conned themselves into believing a falsehood. They are not the sole proprietor of moral values.

This may bring you to ask, "If both sides claim to adhere to moral values, what is it about conservative (or MuscleHead) values that make them different?" Well, let's start with the largest idea, and work our way down to the smaller details.

The Difference That Divides

The major difference between the belief systems of clear-headed, commonsense MuscleHeads and those who are not, in a nutshell, goes as follows: A MuscleHead, or a commonsense conservative, understands and believes that *there is* a God. Many liberals, by contrast, believe that *they are* God.

Liberals usually balk at this. They often turn red-faced and get angry at someone who makes mention of this difference out loud. But it is true nonetheless. This is the single most important idea that separates the two camps. But let me get more specific. When MuscleHeads say they believe in God, what do they mean compared to what liberals say?

Well, MuscleHeads believe certain things about God that are definable. They believe, for example, that God exists in the form of a person or persons. They believe that God is larger than their world, their universe, their own existence. They believe that, contrary to what public schools try to pass off as knowledge about the origin of this universe, God created this planet, the sun, the moon, and the stars.

Most importantly, they believe that God is the source of truth. They believe that because He is greater than them, His Word is important. In fact, they view the Word of God as authoritative and instructional for how they should live their life. They also believe that when they adhere to and obey that Word, it benefits not just themselves, but their families, their communities, their places of worship, and ultimately, the world at large.

MuscleHeads believe that God is righteous and that this means there is a need to obey Him. They believe that to not do so is to commit sin. Sin is anything that misses God's standard of holiness. They also believe that God is just, and that when sin or moral inequity is rampant, if necessary, God will bring about circumstances to set things straight again.

By comparison, many liberals believe God is not a definable person, persons, or personality. Some may believe He is a cosmic power line they can tap into at their convenience to get help.

Others believe God is a person who does not have total control over the affairs of mankind. Still others believe that He is capable, but uninterested.

There are also a handful of liberals who will claim to hold to the definition of God as outlined by MuscleHeads. They do this yet still cling to liberal political positions on many issues. In the pages ahead we will examine many of these positions under the strict scrutiny of this God-divide principle and let the light of truth demonstrate whether their belief in their position or their belief in their Creator is the dominant belief system.

There is one last category of liberals as it relates to their belief in God. These are the people who genuinely believe in God as master and maker of all that we know, yet they divorce that belief from any connection to how their vote should be cast. This is a difficult place to be, for the principles they cling to with sincerity get decimated in the marketplace by the very politicians they support.

A person's view of God has serious consequences. Either He truly has control over everything in this universe, or He doesn't. Either He is the source of absolute truths, or He isn't. Either we can trust that He is in control and is the source of all truth, or we can't.

If God is not sovereign over the world in which we live, then He is rendered inadequate in terms of His ability to resolve the issues of the day. So mankind must then take on this responsibility. We must seek out ways to "stop global warming," harvest life through the use of cloned children then destroy them to use their stem cells, and live our sexual lives as products of the "if it feels good, do it" mentality.

If God is not the source of truth, then His Word is also rendered lacking when it comes to its authority. The Scriptures become nothing more than the words of men from long ago, with little relevance to what we face or how we live today. In the search for answers to life's problems, then, we cannot turn to God or His Word, but must turn to mankind's knowledge—not outdated revelations given by God thousands of years ago.

With such a perspective, we can no longer consider moral laws as absolute. Instead, they are merely "good ideas" that shouldn't be legislated upon all of society. That's because truth can never be known with certainty. What is true for you is not necessarily true for me. Instead of absolutes, then, we have relativism.

Now even though some liberals get angry when I describe the God-divide in this way, they have a hard time disputing the evidence.

This should help us see why it is hard for liberals to become MuscleHeads. In order to do so, they must relent of the power held within their belief system. They must submit to God as absolute and yield control to Him. And they must yield to His Word as the absolute guide for all moral decisions.

For liberals the willingness to remain in a worldview where they are master of their own fate is a temptation that is too great. They view those of us who do believe in the greatness, capacity, and authority of God as those who are weak. While we MuscleHeads find it frustrating to be misunderstood in this way, we should not shrink from the task before us because we have a resource we can call upon in our time of sorrow, need, and anxiety.

That resource is the Creator who fashioned us.

These Truths to Be Self-Evident

One of the truly sad aspects of the God-divide between liberals and conservatives is the inability for liberals to even see a difference. They believe that if they go to church, volunteer at a soup kitchen, and give latitude when it comes to moral issues (in other words, show politically correct "tolerance"), then they are a "person of faith." But such "faith" is only skin deep. It's when our convictions about true moral values—which come from a God of truth and absolutes—are brought to the table that we see beyond this skin-deep faith and see the true heart of many liberals. This was made especially apparent to me in May of 2005 when I attended the Personal Democracy Forum in midtown Manhattan.

The seminar was for Internet and blogosphere enthusiasts who wanted to learn how to develop political strategies using new technology. Because the seminar was taking place in New York City, the liberal attendees outnumbered conservatives on a scale of something like 30 to 1.

Weeks earlier I had attended a largely conservative two-day seminar. There, I had the opportunity to befriend a center-left blogger by the name of Chris Nolan, who maintains the blog Politics from Left to Right. On our second day there, Chris confided in me that beforehand, she had been afraid of what she would find at the conference. But now she realized her fears were unfounded. Why wasn't she afraid any longer?

Why? Because everyone had been so nice to her.

When I visited the Personal Democracy Forum, I discovered why Chris had said that. Liberals are angry. They are angry about everything, everybody, everywhere.

At one of the breakout sessions, "Finding God in the Blogosphere," my good friend and fellow talk show host and blogger Hugh Hewitt was asked to articulate the evangelical viewpoint on the panel.

Near the end of the seminar, Hugh made a comment that sent rage through the predominantly liberal group in attendance. He said, in essence, that part of the reason liberals were having difficulty understanding the moral-values voters in America was because liberal leadership (which he implied has assumed the control of the Democratic party) has forgotten what faith in God is. He spoke reverently to the history of the Democratic party and mentioned that the greatness of the party had diminished because it had neglected to pay attention to the moral values of those who vote.

Hugh went on to say that in order for Democrats to regain a major foothold in the political arena, they needed to go back and "learn how to play the instruments all over again." He said they would never be able to clearly perform the songs without a basic understanding of how melody works.

I believed Hewitt's assessment to be a profound, articulate, and beautiful expression of concern for those on the left to once again discover the roots of faith and how it can bring them to a better tomorrow.

What was the reaction of the vocal majority in the room?

Five minutes of some of the most coarse, vulgar, and degrading profanity one can imagine hearing.

As I sat and listened to the objections being raised, I couldn't help but sadly shake my head. Evidently even the hour-long breakout session in a predominantly liberal Internet forum was not a comfortable enough place for liberals to face the truth.

The Supreme Court Weighs In

Friend, as I stated earlier in this chapter, there are exceptions to this very general principle of believing in God versus believing you are God. It is difficult—nearly impossible—to get any liberal to openly admit to this God-divide. But their actions betray their thoughts. We need not look any further than the issue of the Ten Commandments and their role in our country to be able to discern the difference.

On June 27, 2005 the U.S. Supreme Court handed down a ruling that helped to make this God-divide very evident.

This was the same Court that has morphed itself into the most liberal body of judicial history. During 2003–2005, the Court severely limited or impacted the freedoms that America has long stood for. And in the spring of 2005, the U.S. Supreme Court was at its liberal peak.

In two different cases, the Court gave conflicting rulings in an attempt to accomplish two different desired results by the ruling majority on the Court.

The issue before them was a simple one. Can the Ten Commandments—which are "attached" to God—be displayed on public property, such as a courthouse or the grounds of a courthouse? With the nation watching intently, the Court passed down some of the most convoluted thinking ever to be authored by U.S. Supreme Court justices in the majority opinion, and some of the harshest but most precise critique of judicial activism from the justices who dissented. The case that the Court upheld (and permitted public display of the Ten Commandments) was *Van Orden v. Perry* (Texas), and the case the Court struck down (and thus prohibited public display) was *McCreary County, Kentucky v. the ACLU* (Kentucky).

At the end of the day, this is how the nation was to understand the role of the Ten Commandments in public places:

1. We were to understand that as part of our history, they could be displayed and honored in or on public properties.

2. If there was any doubt as to whether or not they were being displayed as anything other than historical artifacts, then they were to be removed.

In other words, if we believed in the Ten Commandments and held to them as sacred, then we were not allowed to display the very laws that have served as the foundation of the legal systems in the majority of the civilized world, including America. But if we did nothing more than view the commandments as a relic from ancient days, then their display was permissible.

Note that it seems there was a bit of selfish motivation in the U.S. Supreme Court's ruling, for it has a display of the Ten Commandments that it cannot justify removing. Yet at the same time, the majority of the Court was unwilling to acknowledge both the authority of the commandments and the deity who gave them to mankind.

While that last statement may seem strong, I was not the only one to recognize that the Court's conflict in this matter deals with the supremacy of God.

In an Associated Press piece that ran on June 27, 2005, the writer said it well:

> Scalia, Rehnquist, and Thomas have all said that there is nothing wrong with government asserting God's supremacy, while other justices on the court believe in doing so would be to the exclusion of Americans of other faiths or no faiths, and is therefore unconstitutional.[1]

So even the mainstream press admits to seeing the divide. The truly conservative justices on the court argued articulately in their dissent that belief in God, or at least the allowance of it, was key to our nation's well-being and should not be discouraged.

Liberals feel exactly the opposite. For fear of pandering to a "God" who might convict them about the beliefs and principles they cling dearly to, they cannot even allow God's law to remain in the courtrooms in which it has been displayed for more than 200 years of our history.

I believe it is not the offense that these commandments might cause to some other Americans that had these justices worried. It is the realization that if someone believed in the moral rightness of those laws that it would ultimately lead to judgment of them, the way they rule on cases, and the way they choose to live their lives through those beliefs.

This ruling on the Ten Commandments reveals that the God-divide in our nation is a deep one, and it is this divide that, ultimately, is the source of the conflict that is ongoing between MuscleHeads and those who are not MuscleHeads.

No Hope of Common Ground

And friend, the issue doesn't rest upon whether or not rooms full of activists feel like they are being preached at. There is a tremendous possibility that liberals will feel threatened by the mere existence of truth, much less a discussion about the source of truth. And that brings us to realize a fundamental reality that cannot be escaped: our worldview is determined by our belief system. When a person believes in an authoritative God, it causes him to live differently, perhaps more reflectively, than a person who believes he can manipulate God for his benefit.

It is the presence of this God-divide that ensures there will be many future opportunities for conservatives and liberals to grow red-faced on television pundit talk shows as they debate the facts on any given issue. The two sides cannot and will not find common ground *ever*—no matter what the issue. That's because MuscleHeads believe *in* God and liberals believe they *are* God. This fundamental difference in viewpoint is what keeps the two at odds.

3

If It Feels
Good, Don't!

Key to understanding the God divide that separates MuscleHeads from the rest of the population is the effect truth and faith have on how we view the events taking place in our society. The recognition of right versus wrong and good versus evil is inherent in the worldview of a MuscleHead. Yet it goes deeper than that.

Part of being a MuscleHead is the ability to not only recognize morality on its face, but to be able to connect the dots in assessing the conditions that give rise to the events taking place all around us. Only when we properly connect the dots can we determine a correct response to the problem, and ultimately, devise a strategy for staging counterattacks against the DDS and hopefully prevent certain problems from arising again.

By keeping the mind engaged in the day-to-day debates over the ideas, principles, and philosophies that run the world, the MuscleHead develops keen, razor-sharp thinking. This is vital as the revolution progresses, the war lingers, and the attacks continue to be launched against all those who stand for values and common sense.

By proactively plotting how we can address problems, we are less likely to be taken off guard by events as they unfold. It is insightful thinking that will enable us to make sense out of events that are bringing confusion and disillusionment to everyone else around us.

Many times MuscleHeads are required to be politically incorrect by shattering what the DDS claims is "conventional wisdom." But there is little that is conventional or traditional about such "wisdom." Instead, it is "groupthink" propagated by the DDS and their many agencies in society.

Usually when the events unfold, the media and those who aren't MuscleHeads rarely look beyond the surface of the problem in order to discern the true cause of it. You'll see what I mean as I recount some news stories from Memorial Day weekend 2005. If we do not take the time to be careful and commit ourselves to being students of what's happening around us, we can easily end up arriving at conclusions that do nothing at all to remedy the problem—allowing it to only get worse the next time it arises.

Kids Killing

On Memorial Day in May 2005, the Lovely Bride and I spent our Monday doing what has become a custom. I spend the first few hours of the day carrying bags for her and hoofing it from store to store in different shopping areas. She spends the evening dining with me at one of the romantic spots in the World's Greatest City. During that same day, in other locations, some right there in New York City, a series of horrific events unfolded.

In no less than five separate events, children aged 9, 12, 14, 17, and 18 became the main characters in bringing about a most violent Memorial Day weekend. Kids were killing, the details were frightening, and the news media could only hold their microphones with dumbfound looks upon their faces. Even police department officials stated that they had seen little like this in the many homicides they had investigated over the years.

Three of these violent incidents occurred in the New York metro area.

She Knifed Her Best Friend

The incident that drew the greatest attention was the sad story of a nine-year-old Brooklyn girl who got into a tug-of-war with her 11-year-old best friend. According to press accounts, the two got into an argument over who would get to play with a rubber ball. As the tension escalated, the 15-year-old brother of the nine-year-old came into the room and separated the two girls from each other. As soon as he left the room, the conflict began again.

The nine-year-old later told the police that the 11-year-old would not let her alone and, in fact, began to hit her on the arm and head. When she refused to stop hitting the nine-year-old, the younger girl walked into the kitchen and came back with a knife she had found on the table.

As she returned, the fighting began again.

The 11-year-old reportedly tore the younger girl's shirt. At that point the younger girl plunged the knife into the chest of the older girl. Adding to the drama of the situation, according to police, the five-year-old sister of the victim was in the room and witnessed the final moments of her big sister's struggle for life.

According to a report that ran in the *New York Post,* police investigators leaving the girl's apartment were visibly shaken by the brutality of the attack as well as the ages of both the victim and the killer. One officer who had to step around the puddles of blood in the hallway said, "I've been on the force fifteen years, and I've never seen anything like this."[2]

She Choked Her Mom

Just a few miles away on Long Island, another argument turned terrifying and deadly. According to *New York Newsday*, the struggle started out quite simply.[3]

A 45-year-old mother told her 12-year-old daughter to clean her room shortly before midnight. The request was met with resistance and an argument ensued. It soon turned violent—fast.

Detective Sergeant Dennis Barry of the Nassau County homicide squad said the girl wrapped her hands around her mother's neck and choked her until she became unconscious. When the girl realized what she had done, she called her neighbor, a nurse. According to reports, the nurse called 911 and attempted resuscitation through CPR. The ambulance and police arrived and took the mother to the local hospital where she was pronounced dead at 12:43 AM in the morning.

In the space of roughly 45 minutes, a 12-year-old girl's life was changed forever, and the mother who loved her was gone for good.

He Choked His Dad

That same night, in New York's Suffolk County, a 17-year-old boy attended a friend's neighborhood barbecue. The boy's father showed up at some point later and, according to police and press reports, was drunk prior to arrival. When the father received a greeting that he felt was disrespectful, he went and found his son and raged out loud about the rudeness he had perceived. In an attempt to minimize the embarrassment the teen boy no doubt felt, he tried to get his dad to calm down.

What ensued was an argument that the two took indoors and out of hearing range from the rest of the partygoers. The two continued their verbal sparring, and the teen's mother stepped between the two but was unable to break them apart.

According to *New York Newsday*, the teen put his dad into an extended chokehold. The dad stopped breathing and the 15-year-old sister called 911 for help. The teen boy later commented that he had held the fatal hold on his dad (whom he was named after) in order to prevent his dad from further striking him. The family, including the teen, came away completely devastated. Neighbors described the boy as a quiet kid who often rode his bike with his sister.

"He's just always been very sweet, very respectful," said a long-time neighbor.[4]

Neighbors also told investigators that the father was not a heavy drinker and was not usually drunk. Others described the family as one that was close and went to church regularly together.

He Shot Them All

It was Sunday morning of the holiday weekend in Bellefontaine, Ohio. His family had arranged for his picture to appear in the *Examiner* newspaper that day to congratulate him on his graduation scheduled for that afternoon.

But that morning, on the day he was to graduate from school, Scott Moody, an 18-year-old, walked half a mile to his grandparents' house and carried out the first part of what would end up being a killing spree in which he would take his life. He shot his grandparents with his .22-caliber rifle, and then headed home. There, he went from room to room and shot his mother, his teenage sister, and two friends before killing himself.

Remarkably Scott's sister survived, fumbled for her cell phone, and placed a call for help.

As I write this, those investigating the shooting are still perplexed as to what caused this otherwise "clean-cut boy who wanted to be a farmer" to go on a killing spree. And according to CBS *News*, "no one had seen any indication Moody was troubled."[5]

They Kicked Him to Death "for Fun"

On this same weekend in Daytona Beach, Florida, two teenage boys took turns on three different occasions going into the woods not far from their homes and kicked a man in the head and beat him with sticks and their fists until he died.

The boys were 14 and 18. When they were confronted by authorities, according to ABC *News*, they stated that they attacked the man "for fun" and "to have something to do."[6]

The man was 53 years old. He was homeless. And unfortunately for him, he was in the wrong place at the wrong time.

But Where Did It All Come From?

On Tuesday, after the Memorial Day weekend was over, I was on my way to the studio to get a jump-start on the week and catch up on whatever I might have missed by way of news prior to going on air. I was about two or three minutes away from the station when I heard the first of the five "kids killed" stories.

My first reaction to the account about the nine-year-old in Brooklyn who stabbed her best friend over a rubber ball was one of visceral sickness. I thought to myself, *I wouldn't want my nine-year-old daughter to see this acted out on a crime documentary on television. I wouldn't want her to see it played out on one of those made-for-TV movies. I wouldn't want her to see it in a movie theater on a big screen. I wouldn't want her to see such a crime, in person, occur to a person she didn't know. I wouldn't want her to be in the room seeing it as it happened to her sister (as was the case for the five-year-old). And I wouldn't want her to see it happen to her best friend.*

Did you notice the above-mentioned scenarios began at the least personal level and progressed to the most personal? A nine-year-old has no business seeing this kind of violence at *any* level. It's just not right for a child to be exposed to such cruelty at the innocent age of nine, five, or 11. Even worse was that the nine-year-old girl had thuggishly murdered her best friend over *nothing more than a rubber ball*.

As I was walked briskly into the office, I turned to my producer, Gary Villapiano (affectionately known as "V-man" around the WMCA MuscleHead studios), and said, "Gary, I want all the info we can find on the Brooklyn girl story."

"You know there are others, don't you?" came the reply.

"What do you mean?" I asked. At first I thought he meant that the girl had stabbed more people in the panic or aftermath of stabbing her friend.

"No, Kev," Gary replied. "It's everywhere today. Bronx, Long Island, Ohio, even Florida. The kids went crazy."

The sick, sinking feeling I had felt in my stomach from the Brooklyn story now intensified. For the rest of the morning I acquainted myself with the lives and circumstances of each of these children and tried to figure out if the three-day weekend had seen greater loss of life between family members and friends than among soldiers in Afghanistan and Iraq.

But there was no logical explanation—at least, not on the surface. Instead, there was only the numbing realization that we needed to take time to try to "connect the dots" behind this deadly cycle of violence and figure out why it had happened.

Before we do this, let me share a quick side note. I'm always irked when the news media of our day insists upon reporting everything they think is news *except* the news. Apart from the Brooklyn girl's story, none of the killings were given any prominence in the New York media. The national news media mentioned both the Brooklyn girl and the Ohio graduate stories on their 24-hour news Web sites, but neither appeared as major headlines. That's unfortunate, because cumulatively, the five stories hold a valuable lesson for all of us.

In the opening moments of my radio show that day, I told the stories of each of the kids who had killed. Because three of the killings took place in nearby areas, you could almost feel the emotions and tension building up immediately.

The phone calls began to fly into the show with all kinds of comments. But there was only one idea I wanted to explore that day. As a MuscleHead, I believed it to be important to use this particular day to do a bit of careful examination. I wanted to test the waters and see if anyone else would hit upon the possible origin of this behavior. No one did. As I told each of the five stories during the first hour, I told my listeners that at the beginning of the second hour I would let loose with my opinion on whose fault I truly believed these deaths to be.

As we opened the phone lines at the beginning of the second hour, we were inundated by outraged listeners. Some wanted the death penalty for the older killers. Others expressed brokenhearted compassion over the damage done to the life of the nine-year-old girl from Brooklyn, not to mention the sadness being experienced by the family of the 11-year-old.

Making Sense of What Happened

"My friends," I started at the beginning of the second hour, "this was not the kind of day or show I was expecting to experience following a lovely weekend with the Lovely Bride… yet here we sit."

I knew that, for the most part, what needed to be said was likely going to offend a great number of listeners. I knew many of these listeners go through life working hard at their jobs, attending church a few times a year, and maybe even possibly volunteering their time to worthy causes or raising money for overseas relief organizations. In general, they believe themselves to be good people. They would never condone the rampage that had just taken place. But the truth of the matter was, we could only blame ourselves for what these kids had done.

How did I come to this conclusion? Through lofty, philosophical analysis? No. Our society and our families have been living out a morally degenerative worldview before our children for the last couple generations.

You may not like what I am about to say. It may make you angry at first. But after some careful thought, I trust you will see how much sense this explanation makes.

The Rejection of Absolutes

The truth is, we are a society that has slowly given in to ideas that, in the 1960s, were deemed radical, but today have become the norm. The most dangerous of these ideas was, "If it feels good, do it."

This mentality has become more and more pervasive and widely accepted, and has brought about some very serious consequences to our society. There is no question this idea has had an enormous impact on the culture at large.

In the early 1960s, with the advent of "free love" and the throwing off of all that was thought to be provincial and traditional, young people promised to show society a new way of not only getting through life with less guilt but doing so while imbibing as much alcohol, drugs, and sex without commitment that one could find in life. Rules and traditions were thought of as unenlightened absolutes and were thrown right out the window. Churches were about the least "cool" place to be. Faith was an anathema and God was for losers.

In this environment, morality became "whatever is right for you." It is also worth noting that "whatever is right for you" didn't have to be "whatever is right for me." This kind of relative thinking said the only rule was that there were no rules. A person's moral values were whatever one felt personally inclined toward. This required society to become permissive, which it did. Lack of restraint to one's own appetites became the new enlightenment. And since it would only be a "downer" if somebody did bring up limits, you could safely wager that few people did.

The "If it feels good, do it" movement became hugely significant in two ways. First, it helped give birth to the modern feminist movement. And second, it reduced the definition of mankind to the sum of our impulses. I will deal with the effect of modern feminism on our current conditions in a later chapter. For now it is important for us to focus on the second issue: redefining human nature to pure impulse.

What the 1960s radicals gave their generation was limitless appetite—especially for sex. At the time the prevailing thought was, "If you feel like hooking up with someone based on pure animal chemistry—even if you have no idea what their name is or where they're from—why should society stand in your way?" Tragically, venereal diseases began to spread rapidly and new strains became evident during this period of time. This, of course, would also give us the foundation for where we now know the first HIV/AIDS cases stemmed from in North America.[7]

But that's all hindsight now.

The rejection of absolutes—of biblical right and wrong—now transcended our society. This rejection also included our society's basis for "simple morality." I define simple morality as "that which I know is right or wrong based on the thing inside of me known as a conscience." Most of the time, if a person follows his or her conscience, he or she can come to some degree of moral clarity on most issues. Scientists don't have an explanation for how conscience works, but it does. The problem is that the "if it feels good, do it" voices did all they could to remove simple morality from the equation.

Ultimately if you live as a person who is reduced to doing whatever feels good, then a lot of what you do will be nothing more than impulse living. What's more, such an approach to life allows you to throw off the voices that make you feel guilty about immorality: your parents, the church, the community, and so on.

The Consequences of "No Rules"

However the rule of "having no rules" couldn't be set in stone, so a nuance of "morality" had to be defined. So the philosophy was slightly modified: "If it feels good, do it—as long as nobody else gets hurt." The downside of this nuance is that God gave us absolutes for a reason. He explained right and wrong to us for our good. No matter how hard we try, when we reject absolutes, there are going to be serious consequences. People *are* going to get hurt. Permissive sex alone has led to an explosion of sexually transmitted diseases, broken marriages, broken families, promiscuous teens, and much more.

Let us consider one of the major consequences of permissiveness. By 1973, many within the modern feminist movement insisted upon the right to engage in the same type of illicit sexual behavior that men had during the 1960s. The only problem was that this led to many unplanned pregnancies. Such pregnancy brought with it stigma, especially for those who were unmarried. Birth brought with it burden and responsibility, and these were incompatible with allowing one to "do it" if it felt good to them. You can't go slummin' in the bars till the early hours of the morning if you have a baby who needs sleep, midnight feedings, and care in general.

How could this "unfair" burden of pregnancy be equalized so that the feminists could live like the men they so much wanted to be the same as?

Abortion! "Legal, safe, and in abundance" is what the activists sought to create. And, when *Roe v. Wade* was handed down, the nuanced morality became, "If it feels good, do it. Try not to hurt anybody in the process. And if you get pregnant, we'll just stop calling that unborn child a person so you won't feel guilty about aborting it."

The progression—or digression I should say—has only deepened since then. Partial-birth abortion, escalating divorce rates, the legalization of sodomy, the lack of prosecuting those guilty of statutory rape, and the attempt to change the definition of marriage are all part of the furtherance of the mindset of "If it feels good, do it."

The generation who had self-indulgent, nonjudgmental sex in the "If it feels good, do it" age is now a generation of mentors, parents, and professors. They've aged, but the mindset has been passed along in ways more subtle than we think. That's why university administrators look the other way when Ivy League schools know about "naked parties" occurring on campus but do nothing to stop them. (A naked party is where all who attend come in the barest minimum of clothing—college girls running around in see-through lingerie, guys in boxers and speedo bikinis.)

These former "If it feels good, do it" administrators can't enforce a moral judgment upon young people who are engaging in perhaps the same exact types of sexual activity that the administrators participated in a generation earlier. Who are they to judge?

And there are other far more deadly consequences of the "If it feels good, do it" mindset.

In the early half of 2005, law enforcement officials in numerous counties across America issued on average four "Amber Alerts" per month. Children were going missing faster than you could blink. And you remember the stories. Multiple times it's been a pretty young girl who would last be seen somewhere near a suspicious person's house. In some cases, after several days of total mystery and no clues, suddenly a break would occur and the authorities would quickly arrest their suspect. In several instances, the suspect has been a former sex offender who was still preying on children and had harmed the missing child. And far more often than not, that child ended up dead.

Where does a child molester begin to think that he has the right to do what he wants sexually and then dispose of the inconvenient "burden" afterwards? How about the U.S. Supreme Court decision called *Roe v. Wade*? What is the difference between a child molester taking the life of a child that is not his and the abortionist who kills the child that is not his? The frightening answer is very little.

But that is how life looks when it becomes okay to live it on the level of the human impulse. Our permissive culture encourages impulse living in so many ways. And it's not difficult to see how a little nine-year-old who gets frustrated with her best friend will want to do whatever it takes to get her way. Her impulse tells her to use any means necessary.

A Call to Restraint

The truth is, there is not a human alive who hasn't been so aggravated, so angry, so enraged that they haven't felt like doing something they later would have regretted doing. And as long as society is willing to allow life to be lived on the level of the most basic impulses of our nature, we can expect more sad stories like the one about the girl from Brooklyn.

But what if we tried something different? What if, instead of giving in to the most basic animal instincts within us, we decided to take a proactive path that led us to better results at the end of our decision-making process?

While in many ways we've been programmed since birth to give in to our impulses, it *is* possible for us to live more constructively. All it takes is a word we don't hear or even like these days. That word is *restraint*.

Being willing to overcome the impulses that fill our heads and rile up our emotions is a more demanding path to take than simply letting it all out. But it is a necessary part of restoring common sense. We need to listen to our consciences again so that we can begin to return *sense* back into what is *common*.

We as humans have been created with more to us than the sum total of our reactions. We are more than our inclinations. We are more than our appetites, cravings, and desires. But my generation and those that follow mine have not been told this. We have not seen it modeled for us by the "If it feels good, do it" generation.

Our first step to overcoming this problem is to rediscover the difference between right and wrong. The God-divide is much more than a chasm that exists between two groups of people who hold to different beliefs. It also distinguishes between whether we choose to reject truth and head down the destructive path on which we live by our impulses, or choose to consider truth, its potential to govern our world with order, and by faith believe that in accepting it we step into a more ordered tomorrow. Restraint is a key part of living out that ordered truth.

We know that the "If it feels good, do it" generation brought about death, disease, marital and family breakdown, and a long list of additional consequences with it. Lack of restraint ushered in these problems and more. That's why one key strategy in winning the MuscleHead Revolution is being willing to say "Don't do it," or "Wait" when our impulses are telling us to "do it."

By disciplining our appetites, we become stronger MuscleHeads. By exercising the muscle called restraint, we build up one or more areas of our lives that today's society seeks to destroy. When we say yes to that which is good and no to that which is bad, we affirm to the next generation that it *is* possible to live with a clear conscience.

So let's train ourselves to say no when we know that saying anything else would be the wrong thing to do.

4

Making Sense
Common Again

Common sense: Some use the phrase to refer to beliefs or propositions that...would in most people's experience be prudent and of sound judgment, without dependence upon esoteric knowledge or study research....[8]

When I was a young boy I grew up next door to my grandfather. He was a cagey old man who had lived through the depression, a world war, and more of life than anyone I knew. At eight years of age he began supporting his family. Life was hard and early on he discovered that if he used his brain he could make a living, navigate himself around some pitfalls, and even contribute to the well-being of his family. He lived his life according to simple creeds. And in his time, even on the worst of days, there was an accepted code of conduct that boys his age just did not cross. They did not dare.

The prevailing mindset of his generation was that certain things were just "the right thing to do." Certainly the opposite was true as well.

Today that sense of what is right and wrong is on life support. The culture does not underscore it. Parents do not see the necessity of instructing their children on this matter. Even churches have a difficult time articulating this. The result that is left is a gobbledygook mess that no one can explain. Fuzzy thinking encroaches upon the most important of issues, and clarity on the big questions seems illusive.

And what is the solution? The academics want to do studies. The sociologists point to political structures that have supposedly failed us. Yet the overwhelmingly obvious difference between my grandfather's world and the world of today can be summed up in two words: common sense.

What Is Common Sense?

The entry at the beginning of this chapter is the Wikipedia definition of common sense. A key portion of that definition is the fact common sense doesn't require "dependence upon esoteric knowledge."

Those academics who promote the agenda of the DDS, congratulate themselves openly year after year on the new enlightened perspectives and opinions they have been able to bring to our world. Since they are able to propagate their philosophies in a relatively unchallenged environment, they are free to disperse their theories upon those who will carry them into the real world. But as lofty as their thoughts may be, they are seldom as profound and memorable as some of the quaint proverbs my grandfather drilled into me when I was but a boy and he was doing his best to instruct me with wisdom for the rest of my life.

Proverbs such as…

- Plan your work, and work your plan.
- If you can't find time to do the job right the first time, when will you find time to do it over again.
- Knowledge is power.

- A little knowledge is a dangerous thing.
- Treat others as you want them to treat your mother.
- If a man will lie to you, then he will steal from you.
- Absolute power corrupts absolutely.
- Remaining humble makes the landing much softer.
- A man who does his best has much less need for the use of apologies.
- A man's word is his honor.

This list could go on for several pages. Every one of these sayings is a nugget of common sense that isn't necessarily deep, profound, or of high learning. Yet the powerful truths found in these proverbs can serve a person well throughout his life. Sadly, such wisdom is no longer passed on to the next generation. Many of the problems reported in today's news stories have their origin in the fact that one or more people simply did not know or honor "the right thing to do."

Proof Common Sense Is Missing

A shining example of the demise of common sense was given to us in the 2004 presidential campaign. Both Howard Dean and John Kerry, in their attempts to win the democratic primary, made consistently patronizing overtures to the ghetto hip-hop culture in America. In their desire to win influence over the young minds that give heed to the most profane segment of the entertainment industry, they bent over backwards to nod their approval to content that most African-American elders would not allow in their homes. Instead of using their positions as leaders in the American political landscape and enforcing the traditional ideas that not all women are prostitutes, not all men are pimps, and there is little value in anything that is saturated in sex and money, both Kerry and Dean referred to hip-hop as an important cultural influence that we all needed to understand better. The implication was that if we were to be truly culturally diverse as a nation we shouldn't shun this "important" means of expression but embrace it. What was obvious to many was lost on them. And many of their followers—in lock step—played along perfectly.

Common sense tells us that many of the messages in hip-hop music don't even make sense and are dangerous. Sexual promiscuity, drinking, drugs, and illegal behavior are exalted. And yet multitudes of Dean and Kerry voters were asked to embrace such nonsense in the effort to "appreciate" cultural diversity.

Of course, Dean and Kerry didn't really care about furthering hip-hop any more than they did the works of soundtrack genius John Williams. The only reason they made such ludicrous appeals was to pander to a segment of voters they believed would bring more support to them.

Here are some other evidences of the lack of common sense today:

- A teenage daughter must have permission from her parents before a school nurse can offer her an aspirin for a minor headache. Yet in the majority of school districts today, that same daughter needs no permission or even notification to her parents before a school clinic can perform an abortion on her (a surgical and complicated procedure).

- In a nation where the feminist mantra is now the default setting on gender roles in society, women are complaining that finding a "real man" has become much more difficult.

- In the spirit of 1960s permissiveness, sociologists and psychologists have taught that children don't need limits. Instead, they need to just "learn things for themselves." As a result, children today lack clarity and guidance in connection with significant issues in their lives, and have much greater difficulty discerning right from wrong.

- The spending of more money on "fixing" education without clear-cut guidelines of accountability only benefited teachers with tenure and did little to improve children's learning.

- Because of no-fault divorce laws, the incentive for couples to stay together has dropped dramatically. Thus, fewer couples stay together, work through their problems, and become better people and parents as a result.

And the list goes on.

So what would the world look like if common sense were recaptured? In short, the whole world would change. People would tell the truth. Children would obey. Married persons would resist the urge to wander. Honesty would rule. Integrity would make a comeback. Character would be king. Everything from business to government, schools to churches, and yes, even you as an individual, would reap the benefits. Using sense for the common good may sound old-fashioned, but the results would be truly radical for the better. Which brings us to the big question: How do we get it back?

How to Get Common Sense Back

The task of putting common sense back into a society that has lost it is a difficult one. Before we can understand how to restore it, we must first recognize how it was lost. This requires us to turn back to the basis of common sense: the existence of absolute truth. And this, in turn, points us back to where these principles began—with God.

After all, where does sense originate from? It cannot be manufactured in a vacuum. This is why it is so important to understand that whatever we feed into our minds is what we will get back in return.

I've always guffawed over the child-rearing experts who tell parents today to allow their children to "discover their own boundaries" from the earliest ages. Any parent with true discernment knows that *mommy* and *daddy* are the first two words a little one learns, and that *no* is the third one a child must learn.

Why?

Because as flawed human beings, we are not capable of making right choices when we are left to our own devices. Instead, we consistently lean toward making poor choices. The eventual goal of every parent is to raise children who are able to function properly in the community because they understand their place and know the limits of what is acceptable and what isn't. The very fact this has to be explained in a book when we are as "enlightened" and technologically advanced as we are is disheartening. Yet it is necessary.

We spoke earlier of the Ten Commandments. These commandments were the foundation of the legal system in America and for dozens of other civilized nations across the globe. Yet the fact there is a debate as to whether it's appropriate for these commandments to even be on display in our nation's courthouses reveals how far we've fallen in regard to common sense.

Common sense is what told your mom to not let you touch a hot stove, to not play in the bathtub unsupervised as an infant, and to do your homework before you were allowed to play each afternoon. In all kinds of ways, sense brings with it a way of protecting and preserving us. It brings order to our lives. None of that can happen without a moral code for us to live by. In this way, common sense and moral decisions are very much related.

Let me back up that last statement with an illustration. It is common sense to tie your shoes before leaving the house in the morning. You may be wondering, *How is tying shoes a moral decision?*

If you tie your shoes, then you are less likely to trip over the floppy thing on the floor and slip off your feet and thereby career down the stairway and break your leg, neck, or back, thus preventing you from working and supporting the wife and children that you are morally obligated to care for. That is just one of many common-sense things you do each day to protect yourself from negative consequences.

There was a time when common sense was, in fact, common. For example, children didn't dare risk showing disrespect to adults. The consequences they faced in generations past caused them to think twice before lipping off to a neighbor, a policeman, a teacher, or a minister. People also used to watch out for one another. The protection of the "common good" was what they sought to ensure. They didn't need the government to mandate such behavior, as Hillary Clinton suggests in her book *It Takes a Village*. People independently sought the best moral and physical safety and protection for the children they raised and for each other.

There was a time when common sense made very clear the expected standards for our communities, homes, and families. We just didn't cross certain lines. That's no longer the case today.

Which brings us back to our question: How do we restore common sense?

Keys to Cultivating Common Sense

We have to educate ourselves as parents. We have to discipline our children. We need to have them active in the participation of our faith. We need to actively engage their schoolteachers and, if necessary, take over the education our children receive.

That's a tall order. It's one that demands much of our skills, hearts, and minds. But since common sense has been lost by generations of people neglecting all of these things, the place to start is by giving birth to a new generation that is a clean slate upon which to build.

If you have children, sit down and start tonight. Pose questions of a moral nature to them over the dinner table. Wait—back that up. First, have dinner with your kids and talk to them. *Then* pose the questions of a moral nature.

My Lovely Bride's father did this nearly every night of her growing up. The Father of the Bride is a huge fan of talk radio, and one of his favorites is Dennis Prager. Dennis is one of my broadcast colleagues with Salem Communications.

His strength as a broadcaster is to cause people to evaluate on a deeper level that which, on the surface, sometimes seems mundane or unimportant. As he gets the conversation flowing, people begin to see there is more to many situations than meets the eye, and they are forced to wrestle with moral dilemmas as a result.

On a regular basis, the Father of the Bride began suppertime with the question from that day's Dennis Prager broadcast. No television was involved, no Internet surfing either—just Dad, Mom, my bride, and her brother. They were compelled to use that muscle between their ears and, based on the moral foundation they had gained through their faith, coupled with a home filled with common sense, they would discuss the dilemmas Dennis brought up on his show.

You can use my show in the same way. Each day, the broadcast is streamed worldwide on the Web. You can plug in at www.muscleheadrevolution.com. We even offer the full 15 hours a week via Podcasts. You can load up on the information and issues of the day, then use your time at night with your kids to mold, shape, and reform their minds, their "McCullough muscles," and teach them how to exercise Sense in a world where it is no longer common.

By setting this example for them, you will lay the foundation for them, in turn, to model the same kind of parental training to their children and grandchildren. You'll be helping to shape future generations.

Without a doubt, sense is no longer common. But we can make it common again. And it all starts with us.

5

Men and Women:
Equal but Different

More than any other question related to the war on culture, I am asked where I think it all began. An honest answer to this is very multilayered. Clearly, the rebellion against the moral order that God created and established began in the hearts of the first man and woman on earth. But when we look at how the culture war has escalated over the last few decades, there seems to be one rather prominent contributor to this cultural chaos.

As we learned earlier, the "If it feels good, do it" generation changed the way society feels about moral values. This same generation also changed the entire worldview of the popular culture by redefining the roles of men and women.

One particularly influential segment of this crowd proudly called themselves feminists. They did so in spite of the fact that they shared little in common with the true historic feminists who brought about equal rights for women earlier in the same century. Historic feminists such as Susan B. Anthony would barely recognize the shape, scope, and focus of the so-called modern feminist movement and the agenda that it pushes today.

Championing True Equality

In Susan B. Anthony's day, a key issue facing women was the right to vote. Miss Anthony worked tirelessly to see to it that the government recognized that the U.S. Constitution already granted women the right to vote. There were other barriers that women in her day faced as well. For example, it was difficult for women to purchase and own land. And the culture at large looked down upon women who were people of commerce, industry, and self-determination. It was Miss Anthony who championed true equality between the genders and got America on the path to truly living up to the ideals and liberties that the founders of our nation penned in the U.S. Constitution.

In 1872, Susan B. Anthony did the unthinkable. She went to her local polling place in Rochester, New York, and in an attempt to assert her constitutional claim that women did in fact have the right to participate in the democratic process, she cast a vote for president. She was put on trial thereafter and was found guilty. But she refused to pay the fine imposed upon her by the court, and according to court records, she was never forced to pay up.

In 1979, Susan B. Anthony was given a very special and widespread kind of recognition. Her profile was placed upon the one-dollar coin that was then used in everyday commerce.

From Historic to Modern Feminism

So what happened to this kind of feminism?

Modern-day feminism is not a true descendant of historic feminism. For example, Gloria Steinem, the founder of *Ms. Magazine* and perhaps the single most visible icon of the modern feminist movement, is often credited with having originated the saying, "A woman needs a man like a fish needs a bicycle."[9] (While she did make this phrase famous, the originator of the sentiment is actually Australian author Irina Dunn.)

This is but one of many indicators that for us to discuss the current feminist movement is to discuss an entirely different subject than the historic feminism that fought for and deserved equality in the voting booth and marketplace. Those who have picked up the mantle and claim that they speak on behalf of women in the modern era have dared to continue the rhetoric about equality when, in fact, that's not what they're advocating at all. What they want is better described by a different word—and to MuscleHeads, words mean things!

Historic feminists did indeed fight for equality, and legitimately so. But many of today's feminists are actually fighting for something else—sameness. On the surface, equality and sameness might not appear to be all that different. If a woman wishes to be treated equal, isn't she, after all, asking to be treated the same as a man?

Actually, no!

Defining True Equality

Equality bears with it two different levels of meaning. According to the U.S. Constitution, all men are created equal. Susan B. Anthony was correct to argue that the word *men*, in that context, is most properly understood as "mankind," "humanity," "man the species." This obviously was not the way the term was interpreted in the day during which Miss Anthony labored on behalf of women's suffrage. In terms of the sexes and the races, this equality includes the right to sit on any seat of a bus, to dine in any restaurant, to travel freely to and fro without fear of intimidation. Yet this is only the bare minimum of what *equality* means.

There is a deeper meaning we need to acknowledge as well. Our nation's founders knew that ultimately, no man could bestow this state of equality upon another man. It wasn't any man's to take away, nor could it be any man's to offer. Those who wrote and signed the

U.S. Constitution recognized that equality originated from God—
who was bigger than them, beyond them, and authoritative over
them. So equality is not merely a political right. It is a divine right
bestowed to all by God Himself.

In practice, then, true equality should never demean someone
on the basis of gender. True equality could never allow one human
being to possess another. And for the most part, historic feminists
such as Miss Anthony made the case, won the issue, and ruled the
day because the discrimination being carried out against women
was obvious, and even simple scrutiny of the U.S. Constitution
bore that out.

Contrasting Equality and Sameness

Sameness, however, is not equality. It's not even a poor substitute
for it. While equality seeks to bring the *value* of the two genders
into parity, sameness seeks to render the *distinctions* between the two
genders meaningless.

Equality argues that though the *roles* of the two genders may be
different, the *value* or the worth of one or the other is never lessened.
When Anthony fought tirelessly for equality in the voting booth,
she addressed the issue of value. Women were not being allowed a
voice in the political arena. Society had established a value on the
thoughts and votes of men and not women. This was unfair because
this meant women had to live under the rule of elected leaders
whom they had no voice in choosing. Society, in essence, said that
only a man's vote had any value.

Sameness tries to assert that society will function perfectly when
we obliterate all distinctions between men or women. For instance,
modern-day feminists would insist that a 5'5" female firefighter who
weighs 130 pounds should never be thought of as weaker than a
6'2" male firefighter who weighs 230 pounds. Even if the female

firefighter could lift double her own body weight, she would never be able to lift as much as her male counterpart. *It is not a statement of inequality to say that one can lift more than the other because there is no truth that asserts that all women can lift as much as men.* What's more, the woman might be much more adept at operating communications equipment and relaying orders to firefighters who are in the heat of trying to save lives in a burning building. The point is this: If a person's abilities were measured on the basis of what he or she can do, the woman could not pass the test for being "the same," but her value to the firefighting team could most definitely be seen as "equal" if she had a role she could fulfill with excellence.

The same is true about the family unit.

Every child deserves a mother and father. Modern-day feminists tell us this isn't the case. They reason that every child who has two adults to care for them, regardless of their genders, should be reasonably fine.

But there are so many problems with such thinking that it's mind-boggling. Without a father, a son grows up without a true sense of what being a man is about. No one has modeled it for him. No one has explained to him in the language that only a father can—as to how he should develop his work ethic, mind his temper, and develop his code of personal integrity. All these subjects can be talked about from a woman's perspective, but they will never carry the same import as a father who is *living out* his philosophy in front of that same son.

Likewise, how does it ever benefit a daughter to deprive her of the nurture of her own mother? How does she learn about her body, her self-image, her confidence, and the ins and outs of interacting with boys, not to mention all the changes that occur once puberty begins?

And that same girl needs a father, too—someone to model for her how women should be treated respectfully. That girl needs to see her father cherish her mother. That girl deserves the chance to enjoy a long, steady, safe relationship with a man who will open the door for her, take her on dates, and love her unconditionally. This groundwork prepares her for her dating relationships, in which the boys had better treat her with the same amount of overflowing respect that her dad shows to her and her mother—or else there will be no relationship.

Sons and daughters both deserve a mother and a father. Both are *equal* in the value they bring to their children's lives, and yet both are *distinct* in the substance of what they bring.

Sadly, the rhetoric from today's feminists has convinced people otherwise. They have so beaten into the psyche of society that people must be treated the same as opposed to equal. I often wonder if we can ever win back this issue in the MuscleHead Revolution.

What Are We Up Against?

Not long ago I had the perfect opportunity to see the conflict of modern feminism at work. You may have seen or experienced something similar to this.

In the spring of 2005 I spent the early portion of a glorious New York City day on the upper end of Fifth Avenue. The finest shopping options in the world were all around me, and it was an ideal environment in which to catch a glimpse of raw humanity at work. The hordes of bodies coming and going from Bendel's, Bergdorf Goodman's, and a variety of other retailers offered a prime opportunity to witness the effects of decades of feminist rhetoric regarding sameness.

From around the corner of one of the stores came a lone man I guessed to be in his early thirties. From the other direction came a group of about a dozen women. From where I was, I could tell that the lone man and the group of women were going to reach the door of a specific store at roughly the same time.

The bewildered look on the man's face said it all. *Do I open the door for them? Do I let them open the door for me? If I do will they say, "Thank you" for the polite gesture? Will they scorn me for holding the door open?*

Obviously he was torn. What should he do?

He opened the door. He got one "Thank you," two huffs, and a gaggle of women who ignored the gesture altogether. Having just been through those same doors myself moments earlier, I knew for a fact that they were heavy. So heavy that at least some of the women likely would have groused and complained about having to struggle to open the doors themselves or even about no one helping to open the doors for them.

But why was there a debate in the man's mind in the first place?

Because feminists have convinced our society that women are the *same* as men, there should have been no issue at all. Those women should have been left to open the heavy doors for themselves. Undoubtedly, this message had been pounded into the young man's head. Yet at the same time, instinct told him it would be appropriate for him to offer to open the door out of kindness.

This incident is just one small example of the way the feminist gospel of sameness has caused a lot of confusion in society.

What Modern Feminism Has Given Us

One major and tragic side-effect of modern-day feminism is that it has convinced both genders of the "need" for them to take on the attributes of the opposite sex. (Again, because the argument is about becoming the same, not equal.) And in large part, the genders have cooperated. The problem is that they have attempted to adopt traits that are unnatural for them and, in the process, have abandoned their own strengths. The result has not been a parity of value between the genders, but rather, a general lowering of the value of men and women altogether.

Men have become feminized weaklings and, like the man on the sidewalk, have become frozen in moral indecision. Women have taken on an aggressive, almost abusive assertiveness that discourages men from extending commonsense kindness and courtesy to them. In an environment like this, it's no wonder the sexes have actually become more polarized from one another rather than comfortable with one another.

Unwittingly, modern-day feminism has actually *encouraged* meaningless and casual sexual relationships between men and women. It has convinced women that it's okay to engage in loosely constructed "sex only" types of relationships because it makes them the same as men. At one time, the downside that kept women from doing this was the biological consequence of it. But with abortion readily available—per the demands of feminists—this consequence is no longer an obstacle.

You may find it interesting to know that in stark contrast to modern-day feminists, Susan B. Anthony railed against abortion almost as vehemently as she railed for the right of women to vote. She wrote:

> I deplore the horrible crime of child-murder.... We want prevention not merely punishment. We must reach the root of the evil and destroy it.... [It] is practised by those whose inmost souls revolt from the dreadful deed.[10]

Anthony's sentiment was shared by other forerunners of true feminism, including Mattie Brinkerhoff, who in 1869 wrote,

When a woman destroys the life of her unborn child, it is a sign that, by education or circumstances, she has been greatly wronged.[11]

Even though Anthony never married, even though she objected to some of the marriages her relatives and friends entered into, she remained firm in her affirmation of the nuclear family.[12]

Forget Masculine—"Feminized" Man Is Here

In 2005, Agence France Press cited a study that revealed how the roles of men and women have changed in recent years:

Macho man is an endangered species, with today's male more likely to opt for a pink-flowered shirt and swingers' clubs than the traditional role as family super-hero....[13]

Could there be a more dangerous summary of where men in general are headed? The article continued:

"The masculine ideal is being completely modified. All the traditional male values of authority, infallibility, virility, and strength are being completely overturned," said Pierre Francois Le Louet, the manager of the agency who conducted the study.

"Instead, today's males are turning more towards creativity, sensitivity, and multiplicity..." said Louet. "We are watching the birth of a hybrid man. Why not put on a pink-flowered shirt and try out a partner-swapping club?"[14]

This is the kind of news that would get feminists to hold up the victory sign. After all, one of the main goals of modern feminists has been to get men to surrender their natural assets of strength and authority.

The story went on to say,

Arnold Schwarzenegger and Sylvester Stallone are being replaced by the 21st-century man who "no longer wants to be the family super-hero," but instead has the guts to be himself, to test his own limits.[15]

Those words portray what I believe to be the most devastating effect of modern-day feminism: Men are becoming feminized and women are becoming masculinized, and this passes problems on to the next generation. And the data is now telling us that such men have no desire to mentor their children.

Think about the implications of this. From the time a boy is old enough to be aware that he is, in essence, a smaller version of his dad, that boy, under healthy circumstances, watches and tries as hard as he can to imitate the actions modeled by his father. Ideally, he learns as much, if not more, about character from watching his father handle circumstances in his own life than from mere words of instruction or correction.

A good father should *want* to be a champion role model in his children's lives. He is wired to slay the dragon during the day, provide for his family, play catch with his son, rock his baby daughter to sleep at night, and in general establish his presence within the home as a pillar of solid support, steady leadership, and fearless protection.

Compare that with the new hybrid man in the aforementioned study. When a man abandons his masculine role, he deprives himself of the joy that comes from being a superhero to his own family. The high-fives from his son, the tight-squeeze hugs from his daughter, and the look of respect and appreciation from his wife all disappear when he abandons the role he was made for. Instead, as the study says, he becomes preoccupied with having "the guts to be himself" and "to test his own limits." Navel-gazing is one of the major side-effects of modern feminist thinking.

The Consequence of Denying Gender Distinctives

The modern feminist message to men has been clear: Question your natural instincts. This message has caused men to squelch not only their natural role within family and society, but even to alter their sexual behaviors.

For example, though people have practiced homosexuality since ancient history, its prevalence in society has become unparalleled. But how could it not be? Remember, the last few generations have been shaped by the "If it feels good, do it" mantra. More and more, people have been encouraged to live according to their impulses and lower their sexual standards. If men are being told they should deny their natural instincts, then they could easily reason, "Why not take a proxy role of a woman in a sexual relationship?" If men and women are exactly the same (rather than equal yet distinct), then there should be nothing morally wrong with men seeking male partners rather than female ones.

Women have not gone unaffected by modern feminism either. Because the goal is sameness, women have been expected to take on the characteristics of the opposite gender. This, of course, has led to some strange and confusing expectations.

For example, in the War on Terror, feminist groups have argued that women should be allowed on the front lines of enemy combat. Even after the terrifying set of circumstances that Private Jessica Lynch endured, these feminists have remained hardened in their belief. And according to best-selling author Ann Coulter, in a June 2003 appearance on *Hannity & Colmes,* one group in fact advocated that until there were comparable numbers of women dying in combat, true equality will not have been accomplished. The feminists, because of their belief that men and women are the same, shrugged their shoulders at the idea that women coming home in body bags was in some way devastating to the future of our nation.

Women in combat is not the only arena in which feminists have pushed their agenda that defies common sense. Women in the workplace have been told to adopt distinctly male character-istics—even the negative ones. Thus many women have become aggressive and ruthless, adopting a "win at all costs" outlook. This has overflowed into their private lives and affected their marriage and families. Increasing percentages of women are also initiating extramarital affairs and filing for divorce.

Women in general have also been told that it's not necessary for them to be at home to nurture and raise their children. They have been told anyone can raise their children in their place— their husband, their nanny, a daycare center, even the children themselves. Because the surrogates sometimes work, mothers have convinced themselves that it's okay to abdicate their motherhood. They are enrolling their children in learning centers and preschool at earlier and earlier ages because some children appear to do well in such environments, which seems to reinforce their thinking, *See, I didn't need to be there.*

The purposeful forcing of sameness upon both genders by modern feminists has caused much confusion not only among adult men and women, but also among their children. Because of the confusion over men and women's roles, children who may be doing well in their academic endeavors are missing out on the best education of all: the examples set by a loving mother and father who are equal before God and man, yet recognize their distinct differences and abilities for meeting each other's needs and the needs of the children according to their own areas of strength. When the distinctives and natural tendencies of men and women are discouraged, kids then flounder in their own understanding of who they are.

Look, I realize that in some instances today it is difficult for the woman of the household to not work. But in large measure I don't believe we should turn the exception into the rule, particularly with young children. Rather, we should strive for what's ideal for our children. Latchkey kids are a definitive result of two parents working. These kids are increasingly confused about what real manhood and womanhood looks like and are lacking when it comes to the affection and guidance that parental love and authority can offer to them. There are too many influences in our culture that point kids toward a modern feminist view of themselves.

Where does all this put us today? I'll be very blunt: The modern feminists have won the public debate over how people think. Do not doubt this for a second. They have won the public-relations battles, the media battles, the news commentary battles, and the political battles. They have convinced society that sameness is equality. They have strongly encouraged both genders to take on attributes of the other. They have exalted the sameness doctrine in the realm of sexual expression so as to deny even biological differences and to indulge the impulses that lead to rampant sexual recklessness. They have masculinized women and feminized men to the point where neither wishes to be what their instincts tell them they should be.

Ultimately, men and women are being told to extinguish their distinctives and abandon the guidelines given to them by some patriarchal God. Common sense has been rejected in favor of supposedly enlightened thinking.

What these "victories" have brought to society is still in the process of being uncovered. Men no longer wish to lead their family and seek the love and respect of their wife and the admiration of their sons and daughters. Women no longer wish to be a loving caregiver (a role that, biologically, she is well designed for) to their children, and women certainly seem to have no use for men anymore.

So what do we do now?

Putting Your Convictions into Action

The battle against the modern feminist mindset is a crucial aspect of winning the MuscleHead Revolution. If we give in to the tyrants who are destroying the fundamental truths regarding men and women, then we advance our own demise. Given the significant ground already occupied by feminists, any attempt to regain lost territory may seem daunting.

That's why it is so important to understand that merely *knowing* the truth alone will not help win the battle. The knowledge of truth will assist you in assessing the situation, but winning the battle depends on you putting that knowledge into *action*.

Among Christians, when it comes to the social issues of our day, the commonly repeated mantra is, "Trust God; He will never let you down." While it's true God will help us, that does not mean God will do all the fighting for us. Permission has not been granted for us to be passive observers while the war wages. We are called to do battle; that is nonnegotiable.

The truth is that God, as the sovereign ruler of the universe, has the capacity to do anything He pleases. So belief in Him is most definitely a solid foundation on which you can stand when the times get rough. Being connected to Him through the study and examination of His revealed Word to us is vital. But friend, the next logical step is to put your belief into action. A key part of doing this is to dismantle the lie that has been promoted by modern-day feminism.

Exposing the Lie

Let's begin with the premise that men and women are the same.

Are they? We know there is a difference when we step out of the shower in the morning. We know that men are unable to carry a child from conception to birth. We know that women are unable to produce the sperm required to fertilize an egg. We know that men cannot produce the required egg. We know that once a child is born, the woman has the most natural and by far the healthiest way of feeding that newborn, which was built into her by the Creator. Men have no such ability. These are just a few of the many ways the Creator has made it clear that men and women are different. He made them equal, but different. They have different purposes and gifts. And He purposely designed them that way.

Based on the truth that the sexes are not the same, we can only conclude that substituting one for another, on many levels, is improper or immoral.

This whole matter of substitutions being inadequate also holds true for the rearing of children. Without question, fathers and mothers are the ones best equipped to love, teach, and care for their children. Those who delegate their duties onto nannies and daycare centers may believe that the children aren't missing anything and that no harm is being done to them. The children may, in fact, do very well. But a home that does not provide children with the nurturing and love that is so powerfully unique between a parent and child robs that child of what he or she is entitled to. The sense of belonging and intimacy between parents and their children simply cannot be fulfilled anywhere outside the family. So yes, those parents who willfully hand off the child-rearing to others are depriving their children of very heartfelt, special things they cannot get elsewhere.

The first step to winning the battle brought upon us by feminists is a proper understanding that men and women are both equal and important in the lives of our families, societies, and nation. And though they are equal, they are not the same. To say otherwise is to foolishly ignore all the special, God-given distinctives that make men and women who they really are.

So what does it mean for us action-wise?

Living Out the Truth

Men, try in every respect to make every day a new chance to be your family's superhero. Fight the evils of this world, slay every dragon, live with integrity, and devote yourself to your family. Be the example to your son that you want him to believe you are. Be the romantic husband you should be to the wife of your youth. Communicate, model, and transform your family by your dedication to being the kind of man every man should be.

One more note while you're at it: Your wife had a hard day, too. Be her personal, private superhero. Take the munchkins out of her hair for an hour. Help shoulder the stress of caring for the kids during the evening. Take her away from the kitchen and kids at least once a week. Give her a reason to wear that new pair of shoes. Listen to her, and remember how many times she sees what is right and only wants you to see it, too. One more pointer, guys, and all I can say is that it really works—footrubs!

Women, let your husband live out his male distinctives. And while you do, cherish those early days with each child. Squeeze in all the hugs, advice, and teaching moments you can while the minds are open, trusting, and teachable. Be a supportive, listening ear. Kiss the owies. And when you see your husband at the end of the day, respond to your husband's love. Respect him in return. You have no idea how much power this will bring you. Your love and respect will only motivate him to work harder to be the superhero your family needs. And when he feels less than super, encourage him with support. Bite the critical tongue if it starts to unravel when your husband is already trying to get himself together. And when something cannot wait, talk to him—don't nag.

And if you're not married and still reading this, do the obvious. Men, open the doors anyway. Shovel the snow off the sidewalk for the single mom on your block. Be quick to use common sense to offer help, respect, and sensitivity where it makes sense. Ladies, same for you. Let him open the door, and say, "Thank you" when he does. He's not trying to devalue you. Instead, he is calling attention to your worth and putting your best over his. He's giving you preference instead of taking it for himself.

Those suggestions merely scratch the surface. The key is to hold onto the big idea of this chapter: Men and women are equal but different. And allow common sense to prompt you to do whatever is right.

Together, commit yourselves to being the living definitions of what a true man and a true woman looks like. There are many who learn more by what they see than by what you tell them.

This, of course, won't answer every question that this chapter will no doubt raise. We could easily require an entire book to address the thoughts I have only started to deal with here. But if we commit ourselves, as MuscleHeads, to the basics I've just described, we can bring about more significant change in the lives of the next generation than all the millions of people who march in Washington, D.C. could ever accomplish.

The power is at our fingertips. The time has never been more important. Let's make crystal clear to others the ultimate picture of what men and women truly can be...and let the results speak for themselves.

6

Words Mean Things

One of my biggest pet peeves has to be the lack of clarity and substance in much of the communication that takes place today. On my show, I constantly have to ask callers to back up and clarify their thoughts and statements. This usually exasperates them, and the reason is simple. People generally hate having to repeat themselves. But to me, one of the greatest drawbacks in our all-too-hurried world is that few of us take the time to be truly clear. This alone would get rid of a lot of the confusion and disagreements in our world. My fellow broadcaster and friend Dennis Prager says often, "If I had to choose between intelligence and clarity, I would choose clarity."

So much of our communication these days has become abbreviated, assumed, distorted, encoded, and silenced that it astounds me that we are even able to get things done anymore. Technology and politicians have added to the mess. So have lack of communication within families, our literary laziness, and less-than-excellent public education facilitators. Sadly, many have accepted this state of affairs and allowed it to stand—as opposed to digging deeper and forcing themselves to communicate more clearly.

The Danger of Unclear Communication

When we as a society fail to insist upon clear communication, it becomes easier for proponents of liberal thinking to hide behind faulty logic and stereotypes than to clear up the inconsistencies or misperceptions that may exist in their rhetoric. For example, allowing someone to use a label incorrectly usually allows them to get away with making a claim that has little or no substance. In this way he can send a manipulative message, and yet make it appear as though he has not done such.

It's liberal thinking that has contributed to the spread of the less-than-clear standards that schools, teachers, peers, and pop culture delight in promoting to our children. It's liberal thinking that puts expediency before what is right. And make no mistake: The road to mental or intellectual confusion is very much connected to the road to moral confusion. It is poor logic and faulty information that make us more vulnerable to wrong moral choices.

How can we keep ourselves from being fooled? By insisting on clearer communication.

That is why MuscleHeads must always advance the importance of both a clear understanding and a correct knowledge of concepts, terms, ideas, and principles. Clear understanding and correct knowledge can help set us free from the ill intent of elites who seek to use confusion as their weapon of choice.

Let me share with you an example of what I'm talking about.

The Practice of Deceptive Communication

In post-Civil War America, the Republican party was, in large part, dominated by American blacks whose freedoms and constitutional protections had just been bestowed upon them. In the Southern states, the organizing committees who put the individual state chapters of the Republican party together included blacks in ratios numbering as high as 5 to 1 over whites. In the years that immediately followed, Republicans won the majority of state offices, and not long afterward, they won the majority of both House and Senate seats in the U.S. Congress. From 1865 to 1875 nearly every civil right imaginable was encoded into federal law— including the right to vote and to own property. There was even a ban on segregation.

Because Democrats detested this infusion of black voters into the Republican ranks, the Ku Klux Klan was initiated and fueled by prominent Democratic Party members.[16] In fact, the National Archives in Washington, D.C. has better than a dozen volumes simply titled *The Klan Hearings*. They document a congressional inquiry into the Klan. Democrat after Democrat came to the floor of the Congress proudly proclaiming the same message: "The Klan is ours, and we started it."[17] They also began carrying out historic numbers of lynchings throughout the South. This very direct intimidation was carried out for the express purpose of getting black voters to switch their party affiliation and to pressure blacks into dropping any and all political aspirations. By the late 1800s, the Democrats had so profoundly affected voter turnout that they began winning races in both state and national elections. Eventually they dominated all three branches of government in Washington, D.C.—the legislative, judicial, and executive branches. They then successfully argued to a Democrat-appointed, Democrat-majority U.S. Supreme Court that the civil rights of African-Americans should be repealed.

One of the methods the Democrats used to squelch voter turnout was to require literacy tests. When you and I think of such tests, we think of simple word tests and sentences such as, "See

Spot run. Run, Spot, run." These tests were far more than that. One was nearly 27 pages in length and asked questions such as, "If you are accused of a crime and brought before a grand jury, how are your rights different than if you were to go before a regular jury?" The voter was then supposed to write an essay explaining his answer.

As historian David Barton said, "It would be doubtful if modern-day lawyers can readily explain the difference."[18]

The end result of this manipulation via unreasonable literary tests was voter suppression. This, in turn, led to the eventual overthrow of a majority party in Congress, the White House, and the courts.

And even though all this is historic fact, how did it come to pass that the majority of African-Americans in the United States now believe that Republicans, rather than Democrats, are opposed to civil rights and contribute to voter suppression?

Somewhere along the line the wires were crossed. Messages became confused. And unscrupulous individuals in positions of influence began to obscure the truth about the origin of the civil rights debate in our nation and instead chose to promote false stereotypes rather than facts. Words that formerly meant one thing were hijacked and made to mean something else. This kind of deception happens everywhere in society today. This is what those whom we call *spin doctors* are so adept at doing.

Let me give you another example—one that's much more current.

The Manipulation of Language

In the early 1970s, the term *homosexual* had a negative denotation in both society and in medical circles. Understanding that the term referred to someone who either desired to or carried out sexual relations with someone else of their same gender, leaders in both medicine and politics saw homosexuality for what it was—a sexual disorder.

But in recent decades, homosexuals have vehemently protested that their sexual orientation is not a disorder, and have endeavored to convince people their orientation is not a moral issue but a genetic one.[19] The rhetoric apparently worked because at one time, the American Psychiatric Association (APA) defined homosexuality as a disorder and encouraged homosexuals to get therapy. Today the APA no longer classifies homosexuality as a sexual disorder.

Another tactic in the homosexuals' battle for acceptance has been the attempt to redefine marriage. Society has long understood marriage to be a commitment between one woman and one man in a lifetime relationship sanctified by God. In marriage, a man and woman beautifully complement one another mentally, emotionally, and sexually for the nurture and growth of children. To imply that two men or two women could produce such a union is not only biologically wrong but intellectually dishonest.

In a short three decades, we have come to the point where, in the name of political correctness, employers are sued for not offering benefits to same-sex couples, and clergy, who supposedly are spokesmen of the Bible, which condemns homosexuality, are concocting revisionist understandings of Scripture and twisting God's truth in order to come up with some degree of "sanctity" for same-sex couples. In less than 30 years, then, homosexuality went from being a sexual disorder to being politically correct and "biblically acceptable."

How did this happen?

One way was through the manipulation of language. The term *homosexual* has been de-emphasized with a preference for the word *gay*. A term that had previously been used to speak of happiness now provided a more attractive cover for a sexual orientation many are uncomfortable with or find repulsive.

In recent years, the term *lesbian chic* has become connected with trendsetting style. And a more recent hijacking of language in order to make homosexuality more palatable is seen in the use of the term *same-sex marriage*. Marriage, by definition, can never consist of two people of the same gender because such a relationship violates the design, intent, meaning, and purpose of marriage.

In reality, the term *same-sex marriage* is an oxymoron. And it bothers me intensely that good people, who seek clarity in their own lives, have sometimes capitulated on this term. Some of the godly Christian leaders I work with in New York and Chicago—and even across the nation—have succumbed to the literary devices that are placing a cloak of acceptability upon a problem they have spoken out against all through their years of ministry because the Bible speaks out against it.

And I admit sometimes I too have succumbed.

That's why today my producers are free to correct me, even on the air, if I use the oxymoron *same-sex marriage*. While it is convenient to use the term *same-sex marriage* for the sake of time, to do so is to contribute to the confusion that homosexual activists initiated. They *want* marriage redefined. But it's more accurate for us to state their agenda for what it really is: the attempt to redefine *marriage* to include same-sex sexual unions.

That, of course, shows the downside of clarity. Sometimes it makes you wordy. Sometimes, out of impatience, we just give in and use our ideological opponent's terms because it seems more efficient. But MuscleHeads know that to give an inch will result in giving a mile.

If an entire generation begins to associate marriage with the idea that there's really nothing more to it than just saying some sort of vows to each other and having sex regardless of the gender of your partner, then the resistance to changing the definition of marriage in the law becomes greatly relaxed.

Responding to Deceptive Communication

It took only a few generations for many American blacks to look to Democrats as the party that they now must all vote for in lockstep if they are to be properly taken care of—only a few generations removed from the lynchings, murders, rapes, and the intimidation of the KKK. The black community has now embraced the party that used the KKK to suppress their political voice, and this support has been better than 85 percent in the last two national elections.

What is the answer to this kind of hijacking and deceptive use of words?

Insist upon clear communication. When you interact with others, don't yield to manipulation via misused words and false stereotypes. That is exactly what your opponents want you to do. I have my program producers prompt me when I inadvertently use the terms *gay marriage* and *same-sex marriage* in reference to homosexual unions. This also applies to the debate over border security that bubbled up in the spring of 2006. People all across the nation who were organizing rallies in support of illegal aliens kept being referred to as immigration advocates, yet getting people to immigrate *legally* was the furthest thing from their mind.

So, slow down when reading news stories or listen to or watch news broadcasts. Ask yourself, *Does what's being said really match up to reality?* When it doesn't, and you detect someone hijacking the real meaning of a term or issue, speak up. My radio listeners have, on multiple occasions, lit up the phone lines of the *New York Times* editorial desks over the wholesale kidnapping of words used in the course of a specific debate. We should not be afraid to make people accountable for using words correctly and addressing issues properly.

To effectively win the war over the meaning of words, it is important to begin early. Read to your MuscleHead offspring and help them cultivate a love of words and definitions from an early age. And as they get older, train them in the art of discernment and careful thinking. Expose them to the radio broadcasts and writings of commentators who unveil the fallacies of liberal thought. And in time, you will enjoy the confidence that comes from knowing that your child's mind is like a finely tuned machine and that he or she is ready to decisively cut his or her way through today's literary clutter and confusion, stand on his or her own two feet, and be a beacon of light that others can look to with trust.

7

Conservatism—It Already *Is* Compassionate

The liberals' assertion that it is actually liberals who are compassionate—and not conservatives—is without question one of the most misunderstood aspects of contemporary politics. On a regular basis, liberal TV pundits slam conservatives on the issue, and conservatives look wide-eyed right back into the camera and gasp for air as though they've just been sucker-punched.

That ends today.

The debate over compassion is one that liberals have thrived on for a long time. For they, as they tell it to voters, claim liberals are the true purveyors of compassion. When a person listens to liberals speak of compassionate acts—such as caring for the poor, housing the homeless, feeding the hungry, and providing medicine and health care for those without—that person could easily come to the conclusion that liberals are the only game in town.

The fault for this is twofold:

1. Liberals have repeatedly beaten up conservatives on this issue in the press, on television, in print, in debates, on the stump, and in just about every other place possible.

2. Conservatives have let them.

The first problem is one conservatives can do little about. Liberals have few standards when it comes to reasoning or telling the truth, so it's not really any surprise that they would alter the facts. It should also be no surprise that they attack with such ferocity, for they have faced such little resistance up to now. It is the second problem that MuscleHeads can do something about. In fact, they already are.

The Facts Behind the Rhetoric

It is absolutely essential that MuscleHeads pay attention to this matter of compassion. It has been one that has swayed large numbers of voters away from candidates that many of the voters would have otherwise voted for. And sadly, the arguments used by liberals to encourage this sway have been based on deception.

For years, liberals in America have made the issue of compassion to be their domain and have slammed conservative administrations for budget cuts to areas of federal government oversight that assign tax dollars to the funding of these "compassion projects." They have stopped at nothing less than referring to cuts in public funding for school meal programs as the moral equivalent of starving kids. Cuts in spending on welfare programs are alleged to be coldhearted attacks against the poor.

How do liberals justify these kinds of claims?

By narrowing the argument to a specific grid, and then virtually ignoring the rest of the empirical evidence. To their credit, they have mastered this method of manipulating the facts and they have beaten conservatives over the head with it for years. When liberals refer to acts of compassion, their definition is a very narrow one, and it goes something like this: *Compassion is the use of public monies to attempt to solve many of the humanitarian and sociological ills of our society.*

Such a mantra sounds good on the surface. After all, shouldn't a free society be prosperous enough to eliminate such a thing as, say, poverty?

While the answer may seem simple, it's not. The dilemma with poverty is people. It has always been, and it always will be. In the grand scheme of things, the individual is always responsible for the life that he or she lives.

For example, gaining a free education in a free country is one huge benefit that the majority of the world does not enjoy. And this benefit should be a significant step for most individuals toward a free, productive, and responsible life upon graduation from high school. Completing one's training, however, is always dependent upon the individual. Gaining a relatively low-cost higher education or specialized vocational training is another tremendous opportunity that anyone in America can achieve, given some effort. Again, the onus resides within the individual to complete that education or training. In addition, the employment market in America is more wide open than in any other nation on the planet. In fact, large numbers of people come into the United States illegally to take jobs no one else will. Or so we are told.

Given the opportunities for a free education and for professional job training, and the fact that we have so many jobs that people will break the law to get them, those who are born in this country have many options in regard to finding a way to sustain their life. Now, I realize some people are out of work with good reason and genuinely have a hard time finding a job. This is especially true as certain occupations are phased out by changes taking place in the business world. But still, people can, to a very large extent, find more opportunities here in America than anywhere else on earth.

But the key to it all is the ethic of the individual.

And what about those who fall between the cracks? This is where the true debate about what compassion should look like begins to take place. But let's be really honest before we go any further: Some people are lazy. Employers' biggest issue in the workplace is complacency, not overachievement. Even the Bible anticipates the issue of a man's unwillingness to work. Society is told how to deal with such a man: Don't feed him! (2 Thessalonians 3:10).

However, as we observed earlier, not everyone is lazy. Some really are destitute for legitimate reasons. So what is the compassionate response to those facing poverty, homelessness, hunger, cold, and unemployment? Liberals believe in the power of the government to answer the problem. Conservatives believe in the power of the individual.

Contrasting the Proposed Solutions

Liberals believe that an ever-increasing amount of tax dollars should be set aside to house, feed, clothe, and care for those in need. Conservatives believe in training that helps individuals get back on their feet and become able to house, feed, clothe, and care for their needs on their own.

Liberals benefit by promising to solve the problems of the poor by offering to throw more and more tax dollars at them. The benefit to liberal officeholders is simple. They gain constituents from both the agencies developed and the people who become dependent upon the government handouts.

Conservatives benefit in different ways through their reform efforts. MuscleHeads take great delight in seeing formerly dependent individuals become empowered and begin to make contributions back to the society around them. These individuals do not necessarily become a voting block for conservatives in particular because the more empowered an individual becomes, the more he or she acts independently.

Liberals, in essence, gain political power by supporting legislation and policies that keep the poor in poverty and dependent upon the government. Conservatives, in essence, take a chance on losing political power by creating greater numbers of independent and self-sustaining individuals who participate fully in the political process.

Generally speaking, the facts of the case are these:

1. Both liberals and conservatives truly care about those who have fallen through the cracks.
2. Their solutions for helping these people and dealing with poverty are distinctly different.

While both liberals and conservatives are sincere in their attempts to address the problem, liberals are advocating an irresponsible approach to reaching a solution, and conservatives are demanding accountability.

We will look at this more closely in the chapter on taxes, but let it suffice to say for now that MuscleHeads cannot bring themselves to allow the government to, in essence, "tax its way" out of poverty. The liberals' approach of taxing ever more—and particularly in unfair percentages those who are more successful—is for all practical purposes legalized theft. Their excuse, of course, is, "But it will help feed the poor."

When an individual has worked his or her way through the educational and employment ranks to become the financial success that he or she has the capacity to become, the moral position of society should be to not interfere with his or her stewardship of those funds. In fact, the government should honor such an individual's productivity. It is astute business people with money who create jobs for the rest of us. If we overtax those who help start businesses and create jobs, we will deprive them of money that could potentially be income for others. We lessen their ability to contribute to the rest of society in multiple ways.

When the government usurps an individual's rights by seizing an increasing share of his earnings, it throws a monkey wrench into the scenario on several different levels:

1. His earnings are lowered, thus requiring him to work longer hours to make the same amount of money. This also means more time away from his home and family.

2. He has less money to contribute to the charities, community organizations, or causes that he believes in, thus creating a deficit in the good work these organizations do.

3. His money ends up going toward organizations that violate his spiritual ideals. For example, continued federal funding for Planned Parenthood makes every prolife taxpayer guilty through association of the taking of every innocent human life in Planned Parenthood's abortion facilities.

There are more ways high taxation hurts those who are in the higher income brackets, but these are the most pronounced effects.

No Need to Say "Compassionate Conservative"

When Governor Bush ran for president in 2000, he proclaimed the term "compassionate conservative" at seemingly every opportunity. There are many things I applaud President Bush for, but this is not one of them. I felt at the time—and still feel—that the term is redundant. After all, by and large, conservatives already *are* compassionate. I suppose that in order to make a distinction for voters, then-Governor Bush felt he had to argue that his brand of conservatism was in some way different than that of our founding fathers and other giant men of character who had served before him.

But for Bush to add the word *compassionate* in front of the word *conservative* implied there was something wrong with the definition of *conservatism*, and that it needed to be tweaked to convince people that what liberals had been saying about conservatives lacking compassion wasn't true. The moment Bush coined the term and put it into use, it seared into most people's minds the idea that previous to him, conservatives had lacked compassion.

I'm not upset at the president; I just feel he didn't do conservatives any favor by using the term. In the end he won the election, and he kept the promises made during his campaign. That alone is a mighty big accomplishment. He did what he felt was important to do to win the election within the boundaries of good taste and moral ethics, and for that we can overlook him mislabeling millions of American conservatives who never needed the adjective *compassionate* put in front of who they are.

The Compassion Scorecard

For those who doubt that conservatives and liberals really are different in how they show compassion toward the poor, the indigent, the homeless, and the hungry, here is some powerful evidence.

The Example Set by Our Nation's Leaders

During the run up to the 2004 election, the matter of dealing with poverty was one of the many talking points John Kerry sought to inject into the national debate. Keep in mind that the further left a politico is, the more he or she believes in government fiat in regard to giving out the entitlements that they get elected on.

In fact, the reason candidate Howard Dean rallied so much support is that he spoke to the concerns of unmarried single moms, who comprise the single biggest demographic that vote for leftists in America. Many of them look to government to be their husband and the father of their children. They liked what he said about federal assistance. While there's no question unmarried single moms need our help, more handouts of money are only a temporary and expensive solution. It creates a dependency upon federal money that's unhealthy. Surely there are better ways to help unmarried single moms with solutions that have a longer-lasting impact and actually *empower* these moms to better their lot in life.

But while Kerry, Dean, and other liberals did a good deal of *talking* about the poor in the election cycle of 2004, they did little else. They didn't do much to back their rhetoric. Tim Rogers over at the Broken Masterpieces blog was the first to bring to my attention that John Kerry's years of personal giving to charitable organizations formed such a tiny portion of his own wealth that you needed a microscope to find it. And in two of the five years before 2004, according to Kerry's own tax returns, he had made *no* charitable contributions to organizations dealing with poverty. Nonetheless, just like Dean during the primary, Kerry was shown on television making appearances in soup kitchens in America's inner cities. He took the opportunity to be seen in places where the poor are great in number. And because TV cameras were on hand to document his appearances, Kerry got credit for being "compassionate" toward those in need.

In Washington, D.C., just a couple of days before Christmas, quite a different story was played out.

Prison Fellowship, a ministry started by Charles Colson, former chief counsel to President Richard Nixon, had received a special request from the White House. President Bush had seen, only a few years previous, the impact of the amazing work that Prison

Fellowship does in the lives of children whose parents are in prison. One way Prison Fellowship helps these children is by providing them with Christmas gifts through Project Angel Tree. President Bush and his family had made Project Angel Tree a Bush family project on a personal level. The White House wanted to know if there would be a Project Angel Tree "gifting" party taking place before Christmas within close proximity to the nation's capital.

So on a cold, nondescript Washington, D.C. morning, the presidential motorcade drove to the D.C. suburbs. Because this was not an official head of state event on the media itinerary, few media representatives came along to see what the president was doing. The few photographers who showed up concluded this was one of the president's "faith-based things," snapped an obligatory shot of him shaking someone's hand, folded up their gear, and took off.

This wasn't a photo op, nor was it a campaign stop. The president and Mrs. Bush got down on the floor to interact meaningfully with a couple dozen children who had been gathered in the basement of a church in a tough neighborhood.

Every child in the room had one or both parents currently in prison. As you can imagine, this meant their chance of having some kind of Christmas that had any meaning to it was nil. These kids were in the Prison Fellowship Project Angel Tree program, and today, President and Mrs. Bush were the gift-givers. After all the toys were handed out, the president sat and listened and played with the kids as they marveled at this nice man who would give them such presents. Some of the children were not even aware of who he was. The media long gone, the president and Mrs. Bush then had a bite to eat and took time to speak with some of the mothers whose imprisoned husbands made them part of Project Angel Tree.

The entire event took so long that the president's schedule was put behind by about 45 minutes. The nation never heard about what had happened, and liberal radio stations never asked why

John Kerry hadn't had the "compassion" to do the same. And the president continued to endure attack after attack in the media from liberals about how he had failed to live up to his own "compassionate conservative" label. But to him, it didn't matter. The president knew the accusations were groundless. He had, among other things, extended care to a roomful of kids who sorely needed some love that holiday season. Most likely it was an event that neither the kids nor the president will ever forget.

Lest you dismiss that example as an isolated incident, let me give you some other evidence that affirms conservatives are compassionate.

The Example of Two Radio Organizations

As I am writing this chapter, the all-liberal radio network Air America finds itself in deep legal and possibly criminal trouble over an arrangement so hypocritical that it defies description. Al Franken and the other liberals (mostly retired comics) who were hired to execute the all-liberal format are the pinnacle of those who believe themselves self-important to the future of America and the causes they claim to fight for—the compassionate care of the poor being chief among them.

After months of questioning the legitimacy of the War on Terror and accusing the president and his administration of lying their way into Afghanistan and Iraq—and basically calling the conservatives who oppose their viewpoints every name in the book from Hitler to the Devil—a story came to their attention that, as of this writing, they had yet to even address on air.

What was the story?

In recent days, Air America's operation coffers had been enriched by roughly $875,000. This money did not come from advertising sales, or even the generosity of a private donor. Instead, it came from the misappropriation of tax dollars that were intended for the Gloria Wise Boys & Girls Club in the Bronx.

Somehow tax dollars that you and I had paid to the government, which were supposed to help tutor children in after-school programs or fund mentoring activities, with a portion of the money dedicated to the in-home care of elderly Alzheimer's patients, was now sitting in the checking account that pays the salaries of Al Franken, Jeanine Garofalo, and the other retired comedians who make up the daily broadcast lineup. Air America said nothing about this matter and, for six months after they first admitted to knowing anything about the money, acted as though nothing would happen. Then when they were pushed on the matter, they coughed up a measly explanation about how they were waiting for the New York Department of Investigation (NYDOI) to complete its work.

That cover was blown a week later when the NYDOI said that Air America should begin paying back the money, and that it should, in fact, deposit the money into an escrow account that the NYDOI could access to pay Gloria Wise back directly. At the time of this writing, Air America claims to have begun repayment of the funds. However, this admission wasn't made until after Air America had been bombarded for two weeks with phone calls from outraged MuscleHeads asking one polite question: "When will you pay the money back?"

However, even in this repayment, Air America had not yet agreed to put the money into an escrow account. Instead, they "paid back" $50,000 of the $875,000 owed into an account that Air America controls.

The questionable actions committed by Air America were multiple. They preach care for the poor, but somehow ended up with nearly a million dollars of tax money intended for the poor. When first confronted, they denied any wrongdoing. When investigated, they admitted only what they were forced to. And when asked to make restitution, they have "gone about it" by paying themselves back the money they still owe to the boys' and girls' club.

By contrast, consider what happened at MuscleHead Radio over approximately the same period of time.

From the fall of 2003, when we launched in New York, to August of 2005, listeners to Good Guy Radio (WMCA AM 570/970) have raised more than $2.3 million to compassionately care for those in need. Examples of the ways this money has been or will be used are as follows:

- Help feed, clothe, and educate, through one-to-one sponsor-ship, roughly 1000 kids through World Vision, including some affected by the recent tsunami in Southeast Asia

- Rescue roughly 500 "trash heap" kids through Compassion International

- Build 200 new homes for families in the ghettos of Kingston, Jamaica with Food for the Poor

- Send 13 semitrucks filled with food to the hungry in the poorest neighborhoods of Harlem, New York

- Help rebuild orphanages in the Ukraine that were falling apart

- Help sponsor hundreds of orphans harshly affected by the HIV pandemic in sub-Saharan Africa

- Help relocate hundreds of displaced families in the war-torn nation of Sudan

- Help get the medical cures for leprosy to over 120 children who suffer from this disease

- Send thousands of aid relief packages to families affected by the tsunami

- Send hundreds of water purification systems to tsunami-impacted families

- Send thousands of Bibles to Christians in China, Africa, and South America who need them but cannot get them due to religious persecution

- Build three complete church buildings for Christians in India

- Supply hundreds of wheelchairs to those with paralysis in third-world countries

And that is just a sampling.

In alliance with organizations such as World Vision, Compassion International, Cross International, Food for the Poor, Food for the Hungry, American Leprosy Missions, Samaritan's Purse, The Salvation Army, the Billy Graham Evangelistic Association, and many more, MuscleHeads have made a huge impact.

Has the contrast become a little more clear?

Air America, a liberal radio network, got caught red-handed dipping into the till of taxpayer dollars—dollars already earmarked to feed hungry kids and nurture Alzheimer's patients. WMCA AM 570/970 in New York—merely one station out of the many under Salem Communications—asked its listeners to rise up and make a difference, and they did.

And when it comes to comparing liberals with conservatives, this "scorecard" is not an aberration, but very much the norm.

The Example of Everyday People

Millions of conservative people across America attend church services and give generously to these churches and the many ministries connected to them. Many of these churches help to meet the needs of the poor in their community. In addition, many of these same conservatives give to independent charities and organizations that go above and beyond the call of duty to help those in need.

Many of these conservatives have very ordinary incomes, but they give with cheerful hearts. They give to organizations they have checked out and have confidence in. They know that they can hold such organizations accountable for how their funds are spent.

Conservatives Are Already Compassionate

For us to force the redistribution of compassionate care through behemoth government agencies that are not efficient and have no accountability is very ineffective service to the poor. It's far better to support organizations staffed by experts who are equipped to do what is best for those in need.

Liberals have long beat the pavement, the newspaper page, and the TV airwaves with the message that their way of providing compassion is the best way, and that conservatives aren't as compassionate. That's why it is necessary for conservatives to become more MuscleHeaded in their response to these unsubstantiated attacks. Compassionate, caring, people of faith who hold to conservative beliefs have long been living out, for many years, the very picture of what being conservative looks like. What's more, true compassion is, in essence, a condition of the heart. How realistic is it to come to the political conclusion that compassion can be mandated?

Rising to the Occasion

When much of Southeast Asia was devastated by a massive tsunami on December 26, 2004, I was proud to see how Americans responded. Even though the world criticized America harshly for its slow "official" response from the government, still, we responded generously in comparison to the liberal countries of Europe, which have a largely socialist mindset. I knew that America, and the MuscleHeads who dwell within, would rise up and express compassion for the many thousands affected by the tsunami. I even predicted to my wife that when the totals were in, the aid from American individuals would be greater than the aid offered by the government. Some individuals, such as Sandra Bullock and Leonardo DiCaprio, gave a check for $1 million. And many millions of others, like you and I, wrote checks of $25, $50, and $100. Every little bit helped; every little bit counted. And it *all* made a difference.

America's generosity exuded the best of what America is.

Other examples spring to mind. In 2004, Target stores announced it would no longer allow the Salvation Army to ring its Christmas kettle bells outside its storefronts. In the state of New Jersey, 36 percent of the income raised by Salvation Army at Christmastime came from kettles located at Target Stores. This income had to be made up elsewhere. The Salvation Army officials in New Jersey also confided to me that their budget needs had increased that season. Once word got out, MuscleHeads led the charge, and donations in New York, New Jersey, and Connecticut bashed all previous records. In New Jersey, the extra donations not only made up for the shortfall, but went over and above. In 2005, Target once again dealt the Salvation Army a bad hand, and while the campaign to make up the shortfall was not quite what it had been the year previous, still, the funds that were raised exceeded the need.

The inherent desire of conservatives to be compassionate is what makes MuscleHeaded compassion so unstoppable. If a MuscleHead has a full head of steam about a cause, then he or she will often dig deep in order to help. And let's be clear: The average MuscleHead doesn't have a six-figure income like many of Hollywood's elite, Washington's elect, or academia's tenured. Yet it's the little gifts from many people of faith, people who care, and people who think that easily eclipse the large and showy resources of the liberals who talk so much yet by comparison give so little.

Conservatives have always been and always will be compassionate. Choosing to be so is just one of the most attractive—and most important reasons—we MuscleHeads want to remain conservatives!

8

All Men Are Created Equal
(Except to Liberals)

In the U.S. presidential campaign of 2000, there was a great fraud perpetrated on the American voter. It was a fraud that used people of color, manipulated how they were fed information about the events that unfolded before them, and eventually disenfranchised the will of many African-American voters.

No, the fraud had nothing to do with the courts in the state of Florida, then-Attorney General Katherine Harris, or even the Supreme Court of the United States. The fraud was committed by the leaders of the civil rights communities in this nation. From the painful way the Reverend Jesse Jackson took to the podium and repeatedly had audiences chant, "Stay Out' Da Bushes" to the way the NAACP deceptively implied that then-Governor George W. Bush had somehow been complicit in the horrific dragging death of an African-American named James Byrd, the leadership of the old-guard civil rights movement in America were divining a political poison that had a deadly intent.

The rumors were whispered, took advantage of the commendable loyalty of the black community, and spread like wildfire. Before long, I was receiving e-mails asking me why Governor Bush wanted to take away the voting rights of African-Americans, why he didn't want to see justice done in the Byrd murder, and in subsequent years, why he wouldn't meet with the NAACP.

Given these thoroughly unsubstantiated accusations, it was little wonder that less than nine votes out of every 100 cast by the black community went toward Bush, comprising perhaps the strongest distrust ever expressed by African-Americans toward a conservative candidate for president. And to this day, uninformed minds argue vehemently that President Bush stole the election, and that he did it by squashing the black vote in Florida.

On the issue of civil rights, liberals have long claimed dominance and superiority. The implication is plain: Conservatives don't believe in civil rights, and only liberals can unlock the doors to equality. The debate has become more confusing in recent decades because what is now considered equality is not the same definition society had in the days of segregation, and especially in the days of slavery. Terms such as *affirmative action, employment quotas,* and *equal opportunity in lending, housing, and employment* have added new subtleties to the fundamental meaning of equality. Add to that mix a Republican president who comes along and talks about the fundamental inequality of the education system, home ownership (not subsidized housing), and the "soft bigotry of low expectations,"[20] and there are even more nuances to the whole matter of what equality means in American society.

Summed up, liberals assert that when it comes to civil rights, they've taken the high ground, and that conservatives are racist and silent on the issue. However, the truth is a gravely different story.

History Reveals the Truth

Let's start with something big. When were full civil rights first achieved for persons of color in America, and which political party ushered in those rights?

Most of us, especially those educated in public schools, were taught to believe that it was the Democrats of 1963—1965. The facts tell us otherwise.

Following the end of the Civil War, there was naturally much upheaval in the political systems within the states as well as the federal government. The Republican party set itself on a course to establish total and complete equality for all persons, regardless of skin color, in the reunified nation.

By 1875, with the stewardship of both houses of Congress as well as the executive branch, the Republicans steamrolled the last of a total of 23 different pieces of federal legislation that established full civil rights for former slaves. These laws banned segregation, granted full voting rights and the right to own property, and banned all the forms of violence that had sprouted up from the newly founded terrorist organization the Ku Klux Klan, an organization started by prominent Democrats in response to the growing power blacks were wielding in the Republican party.[21]

In the former Confederate states, the Republican party charters were drawn up primarily by former slaves. And in an astoundingly short period of time, some men went from being a slave and working another man's property all the way to the halls of Congress and serving as elected representatives.[22] Blacks were overwhelmingly Republican, and were proud to be so.

Out of sheer frustration and anger, the Democrats fought back. The Ku Klux Klan was formed in 1866, and lynchings were instituted as a form of terror to threaten and to intimidate. And in the Southern states, former slaveholders worked hard and fast to make it necessary to pass a literacy test before one could vote.

Only these were unlike any literacy tests you and I have ever taken.[23] David Barton, a noted historian and the founder of the historical preservation society known as Wallbuilders, said the following on one of my broadcasts in the summer of 2005:

> These tests were beyond ridiculous, they were harsh and unfair. One question read something to the effect, "What is the difference to your rights as a defendant if your case is brought before a grand jury as opposed to a regular trial jury?" It is doubtful that many lawyers could get that right, much less former slaves. Yet this was the requirement [in order to vote] that had to be met in some of the Southern states after the passage of these phony literacy tests.[24]

The tests and threats were designed to suppress the turnout of the black voters in the Southern states. One black lawmaker, U.S. Representative Richard Cain of South Carolina, went so far as to say, "The bad blood of the South comes because the negroes are Republicans. If they would only cease to be Republicans and vote the straight-out Democratic ticket there would be no trouble. Then the bad blood would sink entirely out of sight."[25]

The tests created by the former slaveholders had the intended effect. Some blacks stopped voting, and many others decided to forsake the party that had fought for their newfound freedoms. Powerless to do anything else, they resigned themselves to joining the Democratic Party.

The Democrats had lost their political clout in 1861, but after the Civil War, through the effective use of intimidation and fraud, their numbers began to rise. This happened first in the state legislatures, where local laws were often repealed and changed. Eventually, by 1893, the Democrats won back the House, Senate, and White House. They made quick work of turning around and passing a federal law that repealed the ban on Klan violence. In a very short matter of time, all the federal civil rights legislation that had been established by Republicans was also overturned. Democratic majorities in both the House and the Senate passed the bills that had the power to do this, and President Grover Cleveland, a Democrat, signed them into law.[26]

What made this especially heinous was the fact that from 1875 to 1893, African-Americans had tasted freedom. They had enjoyed the right to participate fully and equally in every aspect of American life. But because of the actions of the Democratic party, civil rights were snatched away and remained elusive for African-Americans for another 70 years. During those years, the Republican political platform called for bans on lynching and Klan violence in 1896, 1920, 1924, 1928, 1944, and 1948. The Democratic political platforms to this day have yet to call for a ban on lynching.[27]

Improvement Needed on Both Sides of the Aisle

Whenever I have brought up these historical facts on my radio show, invariably the first caller to make it on the air will be an African-American who has never heard these facts before. Rather than acknowledge the dismal track record of liberals in championing the cause of freedom and civil rights, the oft-defensive voice on the other end of the phone will sputter, "Well, what have the conservatives done for us lately?"

The implication is that under liberals, black people "have been well cared for." Another important implication is that because Republicans have not made concerted efforts to champion the "great society solutions" of the postsegregation era, they must be racist and want to keep black people down.

Neither assumption is true. And let me point out that *both* parties have made crucial mistakes since World War II on how they have approached the issue of equality for all persons in modern times.

What Really Happened with
Civil Rights Legislation

Democrats cite the civil rights accomplishments of the 1960s as evidence that they are the political party of the oppressed. Democrats have also regularly and successfully cast Republicans as "the party of the rich" in the eyes of minority voters. Closer looks at both assumptions prove them to be false.

In the 1960s, America was in turmoil and Democrats were under increasing pressure to deal with the racial strife. Few people know, however, that the civil rights legislation passed in 1963—65 was *not* authored by the Kennedy administration, which merely passed it. Rather, the language and intent of the bills, as passed, were essentially unchanged from when they had been introduced the first time by Republican President Dwight David Eisenhower. Why weren't the bills passed when Eisenhower introduced them? Because congressional Democrats killed them at the committee level.[28]

Why did the Democrats finally change their minds and support the bills introduced by a Republican president?

There's more. The Voting Rights Act of 1965, which guaranteed that blacks can have equal and full participation in the electoral process (a right that Republicans had *already* granted nearly 100 years earlier), included a "sunset provision" that would cause this guarantee to expire 42 years later. Why did the Democrats insert such a provision if they were fully committed to equality? The answer to this shows how Democrats have really viewed civil rights issues throughout the nation's history. This view still holds true today and is one of the defining differences between liberals and MuscleHeads.

Liberals view the government as the bearer of gifts. These gifts enslave the voter to re-elect liberals so that liberals will continue to give these gifts to the voters who elected them in the first place.

This causes liberals to remain in power, for their constituency is dependent upon them. Conservatives, by contrast, believe that the government's primary role is to facilitate and protect the opportunities for individuals to exercise their divinely given rights in a free society.

By placing a sunset provision in the Voting Rights Act of 1965, liberals set themselves up to have a "savior moment" down the road. It should be of no surprise that they would do that.

In August of 2005, leaders of the civil rights community met in Atlanta to excoriate conservatives and imply that conservatives wished to take away the voting rights of blacks in 2007. Yet nary was a word of criticism leveled toward the liberals who wrote this racist provision into law to begin with. Moreover, the criticism leveled at fellow blacks over their desire to stand with conservatives became one of the more rhetorical themes of the gathering.

Rhetoric vs. Reality

In 2007, I have no doubt that America will finally put an end to the sunset provision in the 1965 Voting Rights Act. The fact that this provision was even added is a lasting tribute to the fact that liberals view racial equality in purely pragmatic terms as opposed to genuinely principled ones.

"If a black man is a tyrant, he is first and foremost a tyrant, then he incidentally is black," said longtime civil rights activist Harry Belafonte. "Bush is a tyrant, and if he gathers around him black tyrants, they all have to be treated as they are being treated. Hitler had a lot of Jews high up in the hierarchy of the Third Reich. Color does not necessarily denote quality, content, or value."[29]

That wasn't all. Dick Gregory added, "Black conservatives have the right to exist, but why would I want to walk around with a swastika on my shirt after the way Hitler done messed it up? So why would I want to call myself a conservative after the way them white racist thugs have used that word to hide behind? They call themselves new Republicans."[30]

And not to be outdone, America's chief race pimp weighed in: "Race baiters and discriminators may go underground, but they never move out of town," said the ever-rhyming Reverend Jesse Jackson.[31]

Though Belafonte, Gregory, and Jackson continue to bristle with accusations in the halls of "Groupthink USA," the facts of the matter tell a different story.

Under President Bush, the need for government-subsidized housing in America has gone down. Why? Because black home ownership has skyrocketed.[32]

Aid to Africa for the HIV crisis and pandemic poverty in the sub-Saharan region, along with a willingness to stand up to the dictators and corrupt government officials who are ruining Africans' lives, are causes that this conservative president has championed in ways that no president before him has even come close. And in the area of education, the gap on schoolchildren's reading scores has closed to the narrowest margin in the history of our nation, with thanks to President Bush's No Child Left Behind Act passed in 2001.[33]

None of this is to say or even pretend that Republicans have been perfect when it comes to civil rights. Too many times, Republicans could have done far more to speak out and address civil rights inequities but didn't. Post-*Roe v. Wade* social conservatives have pressed on issues outside of racism and at times acted as though the problems of race no longer existed. Even recent blunders such as the one made by Republican Trent Lott, in which he espoused the great potential a former segregationist would have as president, was a serious mistake—one that the liberal media jumped all over.

By contrast, the press was nowhere near as outraged when a former Klan member, Senator Robert Byrd of West Virginia, a Democrat, was praised by Connecticut senator Christopher Dodd in 2004 as being a man "who would have been right at any time" in our nation's history.[34] In fact, this didn't even stop the newly elected and only presently serving African-American senator Barack Obama (also a Democrat) from sending out fundraising letters on Byrd's behalf in 2005.

The Future of Civil Rights

MuscleHeads, listen carefully. There is no time to waste. The future of civil rights in America is intricately linked to the future of cultural morality. If the culture does not take intense and serious interest in propagating morality, eventually the thought, concept, and fabric of civil rights will be eroded.

For example, how can we argue that a man is equal to another man yet believe that his life has the right to be taken in its earliest stages?

Liberals' acidic views and perversion of the civil rights message have already surfaced in arguments about morality that are being viewed in attempts to shape our society. African-Americans had the right to be outraged at gay activists who try to equate the DNA argument ("we were born this way") with the fact that blacks are born with dark skin. Though there is no scientific proof to support the gay activists' claims,[35] that did not stop the likes of Jesse Jackson and Al Sharpton from proclaiming that such a comparison is appropriate.

So the fraud mentioned at the beginning of this chapter still continues. Liberals sound good when they talk civil rights, but their actions betray their words. And the liberal media continues to hold a double standard when it comes to reporting the facts.

MuscleHeads, we need to take a stand and proclaim the truth about the equality of all people. The most important part of this truth is that equality stems from the One who made us—God. God created man in His image. God breathed life into him. God judges all equally and holds all to the same standard—His. The equality of man is not something that can be withheld or granted.

It has already been given.

For those on the political right, it is imperative that you never again seek to minimize the importance of this MuscleHead principle. For those on the political left, your days of manipulating this issue to enrich your personal political power are numbered. MuscleHeads will blaze a new path: one on which pain is felt when injustice occurs, and truth and strength are spoken to the powerful who seek to deceive.

In the end, truth will win. Truth, when coupled with faith, is always victorious. And MuscleHeads will implement both in their fight for justice in the desire to remind our world that All Men Are Created Equal!

9

The Only Fair Tax
Is a Flat Tax

G iven that this book has spoken largely to the moral crises of our time, you may wonder why an entire chapter has been devoted to the issue of taxation. What do taxes have to do with the moral, cultural, and spiritual issues we have addressed so far? You might even say, "Didn't Jesus say to render unto Caesar what is Caesar's?" That is, when it comes to government matters, we have no choice but to simply keep quiet and comply.

As I will demonstrate in the pages ahead, nothing could be further from the truth.

Not only is the matter of taxation a legitimate plank in the MuscleHead Revolution, but it is a key issue that sits as sort of a second foundation beneath many, if not most, of the other principles we MuscleHeads are attempting to enact into our lives. (The first foundation being "It's God, stupid"—see chapter 2.)

Taxes and Society's Moral Values

The degree to which a society values morality is reflected in the taxes it subjects upon its people. In other words, if a society's tax code is corrupt, many other things in its culture will be corrupt as well.

I know that is a bold statement for me to make, and you may wonder if it's justified. But allow me a moment to peel back the layers of this distasteful onion and explain my point.

First, the Creator God Himself never advocated a tax-free society. Scripture is replete with specific instructions on how bibliocentric people are to approach the issue of paying taxes. The message is simple: Pay them.

But the instruction on taxation, as it is often advocated by "big government" liberals, typically stops right there. It's true that when Jesus asked His followers whose image was on the Roman coin, He instructed them to give to Caesar what was due him. This was an explicit command to pay any taxes that were owed. However, the truth in Jesus' instruction went further than that. Christ was pointing to a much bigger picture—that of stewardship and our participation in the society to which we belong.

As people of faith, MuscleHeads are required to do more than just pay taxes and vote. Those are the bare minimums of what is expected of us. To fully follow Christ's command requires that we do much more. Obviously that "more" will vary depending on the type of nation we live in, the period in history in which we live, and the degree of freedom that we are given. And given that all these factors are very favorable here in America, the implication for all people of faith, for every conservative, and certainly for every MuscleHead, is this: Twenty-first century America is *your* time!

I say that because the government in America is "we the people." And it is vital that we recognize we are the ones who set the agenda, we are the ones who pay the taxes, and we are the ones who write the tax code.

Having said that, I believe it may be a testament to our true material wealth as a nation that riots are not breaking out in the streets over the injustice our present tax code inflicts upon us. We are a high-minded nation when it comes to honoring the equality of man, but when the government (which is run by us) hands out a sentence to each of its citizens that is incapable of being appealed (the amount of taxes each person will pay), we sit quietly and condone the fact that pure discrimination, pure prejudice, and pure irresponsibility is written into federal law.

With such callous disregard for what is equal to what every man must face in this nation, is it any wonder that we segment our thinking on moral issues such as racism, abortion, sexual expression, and the corrupt society we are watching our children inherit?

Tax codes have always been a gauge for the moral temperature of societies. God addressed the matter early in scriptural texts, making sure that the children of Israel brought what was due Him first. In essence, He said, "My moral order comes before the establishment of your civic order." We see this again in the New Testament: Under the oppression of Rome, Christ told His followers to pay their taxes. He said this even though the people lived under a dictator and not in a democracy, and even though Rome would soon unleash horrible persecution upon Christians.

Modern history reveals to us that dictators consistently levy heavy taxes on the people they control. Such taxation is used to execute immoral and oftentimes inhumane regime agendas. In communism's prime, taxes were excruciating and the people who were made to pay them were told God was dead. The state was now their god, and the state would provide for the people's needs.

This is just one way we can see how morality and taxes go hand in hand.

Some Revealing Numbers

By this principle—a fairly universal standard—America is a grossly immoral and discriminatory nation. Because of the checks and balances system our representative republic maintains between the various branches of government, we are not as bad off as those under the regimes of dictatorial states. But for a nation that claims to be governed by "we the people," our tax code defies explanation.

While the numbers shift from year to year, a general rule of thumb is that two percent of our population pays 50 percent of our nation's tax burden. Nearly a third of our population pays nothing, and the rest have a hard time paying the taxes that are required of them.

Let's apply those numbers to the matter of equal rights.

Suppose we let a third of the population have complete civil rights, require two percent to work as slaves under the same conditions that existed prior to the Civil War, and require the remaining people to prove their worth every year in order to be granted the civil rights they desire. How well would such an arrangement be received today?

Better yet, let's apply the numbers to the workplace. Suppose your company has 100 employees. Two of them must work 160 hours a week. Thirty-three of them don't have to work at all. And the remaining 65 must work 60 to 80 hours a per week. And the catch is this: Everyone goes home with exactly the same paycheck.

As you can see, from an equal-rights or employment standpoint, no person alive would agree to the terms that exist in our present tax code. Yet when it comes to taxes, that is exactly what we do. And sadly, there are some in our society who are fighting to increase the unfairness, and they label those who object as being racist, bigoted, insensitive, and uncaring.

Getting It Right Is Vital

If the premise is true that a nation's tax policies reflect the moral climate of that nation, then we should be concerned. If it is verifiable that our tax code is inherently unfair and thus immoral—

as immoral as racial inequality—then we have our work cut out for us. Make no mistake: Correcting our tax code is a vital step toward returning America to its moral foundations. It is hypocritical for us to seek justice in relation to racial discrimination, the protection of innocent life, one's right to own property, and one's individual responsibility to those around us and yet neglect justice when it comes to taxes. If we are not advocating justice for all in the one area that should treat every man and woman equally in their relationship and responsibility to the federal government, then how can we ever expect that the justice needed by some will ever arrive to the greatest degree possible?

Why the Tax Code Has to Change

Though America's tax code is nowhere near the worst in world history, still, it is immoral, discriminatory, and locks the impoverished to a future without hope. It is immoral and discriminatory because it does not treat all people fairly. It requires those who are successful to pay much more for the fewer services they actually need, and allows those who pay nothing into the system to gain numerous benefits for nothing. There is no exchange of equitable value taking place that treats all taxpayers equally.

Our tax code locks the impoverished into a future without hope because those who pay the highest tax amounts become much less able to help create an economic system that nurtures new opportunities for those most in need and rewards such opportunity based on initiative and effort. The more taxes we impose on the highest earners, the less capable they become of using their own earnings to create jobs and unlock economic stimulus, which, in turn, creates greater consumer demand—and so the cycle goes. The impoverished are the ones who need the most economic stimulus. Liberals usually sneer at the rich because of their wealth, but it is the rich who can create the economic stimulus we need. And the fact is, the rich can create that stimulus in bucketfuls. Government, through taxation, interrupts that potential by piling on taxes.

What's more, liberals continue to argue constantly that the government needs to raise taxes, claiming all the while that this will benefit those who are needy. But such a move would actually *accelerate* the disintegration of the livelihoods of the needy. When you raise taxes, you hurt the poor more than anyone else. Both history and common sense confirm this.

Why Is the Flat Tax a Fair Tax?

The major reason the flat tax is a fair tax is that it more or less executes the taxation process equally to all men—regardless of race, color, gender, creed, or social position in life. No one escapes the flat tax, and no one cheats it. Whether a wage earner makes $9000, $90,000, or $9,000,000 a year, he or she will pay an equal percentage. Because it is a universal tax, it treats all people equally—no special favor for anyone nor discrimination against anyone. When you consider that everywhere else in American life we insist upon equality for all, it doesn't make sense to permit inequality when it comes to what the government takes from us for the fruit of our labors.

"But Kevin," I have heard many a person say, "the rich deserve to pay more." Even in that statement—which I don't disagree with—the idea of equality is embraced. Yet when it comes to reforming the tax system to make it *truly* equal, what many of these people really mean is, "I want the rich to pay for it all, and I shouldn't have to pay anything."

But let's take a closer look at the flat tax by considering a basic premise.

Steve Forbes, a true and outspoken champion of the flat tax, has written a best-selling book about it, and is pushing for reform to the federal tax code. He proposes that the flat tax be set at 17 percent. So when your taxes are due, you would figure out 17 percent of your gross income for the year, and send that to the government. No complicated forms to fill out.

The result of a 17-percent tax is that the top bracket of taxpayers would pay about half of what they currently pay. And what would happen to all those dollars no longer going to the government? They would be free to go to the private sector and the economy— buying products, hiring construction crews, building infrastructure, providing transportation, and so on.

And what does the private sector gain out of a flat tax? It gains more new jobs and new capital, which help open up growth for the economy. Because the top taxpayers now have more money to invest, they can hire more workers, give more raises and promotions, and so on. This places more money in the pockets of the private sector, enabling people to buy more goods and services—thus stimulating the economy.

By contrast, when you increase taxes, the "stimulus makers" are forced to make a decision—either add a new franchise location, or pay the bigger tax bill. Either hire new staff, or cut back and reduce benefits. As you can see, the flat tax explodes the economy with positive creative energy and capital. Increasing taxes chokes the economy and tells it that growth is not good.

In the last 50 years, three presidents have made significant tax reductions—George W. Bush, Ronald Reagan, and John F. Kennedy. All three times, the presidents' political opponents called these reductions tax cuts for the rich. All three times, pro-big government liberals squawked about the lack of revenue that such reductions would create. All three times, there were nebulous warnings that the government would lack sufficient funds to help the needy.

Yet all three times, the reductions brought about results that modern liberals won't mention. In all three instances, revenue to the federal government (the amount of money the government takes in from the taxpayers) *increased* in the year following the tax cuts.

Why?

Because the reduction in tax burden to the worker resulted in greater personal wealth. Thus taxpayers ended up sending *more* money to Washington. When the tax burden was lessened, it unleashed the creative power of the economy, allowing it to boom.

Now you may be thinking, *Well, it sounds good, but shouldn't the rich still be forced to pay more?*

The answer is that under a flat tax, they will still pay more. For example, if 10 percent becomes the new standard for the federal tax system, this is how it would apply to the three salaries I mentioned earlier:

- The worker who earns $9000 a year would pay $900.
- The worker who earns $90,000 would pay $9000.
- And the worker who earns $9,000,000 would pay $90,000.

Notice what happens. The middle-class and highest-class earners, in essence, pay the equivalent of the salary of the person in the next level down. And the rich will pay the most, and all the workers contributing to the tax rolls will be treated fairly.

So Why Do Some Fight Against It?

You may have heard the saying, "Give a man a fish and you feed him for a day. Teach a man to fish and you feed him for the rest of his life."

In the halls of the federal government the saying has been twisted to something like, "Give a man a fish and you feed him for a day; teach a man to fish and you put a politician out of work. End political unemployment, and stop teaching men to fish."

The truth is that there is no downside to reforming the tax code and turning it into a fair and flat system, except for one. Liberal politicians get elected by promising entitlements to people. They stay in office by growing the number of people who are dependent upon them to get their entitlements. So a flat tax may put such politicians out of office.

If the tax code is reformed and more jobs are created, then productivity will explode all across the nation. People will begin to buy homes that they have never been able to afford before. They will send their kids to different schools based on the needs of their child and not the availability of programs that are forced upon them.

If we reform the tax code, the government's revenue would actually increase, giving more support to those safety-net programs that are necessary to help the needy who fall through the cracks. Yet the purpose of reforming the code would be to see fewer people fall through the cracks—and that's called social justice.

Clearly, liberals hate the idea of a flat tax because ultimately it is an indictment against everything they have claimed while running for office. In short, if people are able to have more control over their own life, then government is not needed. That wouldn't make liberals happy, for they advocate redistributing wealth taken through taxation and funneled into programs they have convinced their voters are needed.

The moral implications of forcing people to put their tax dollars into specific government programs are frightening. When my wife and I decide to help those stricken by poverty, we research various ministries or charities to find those that are doing their work in ways that do not violate our conscience. For instance, we don't want to help a program that tutors teens yet on the side counsels the teen women to kill their unborn children.

My lovely bride and I currently give regularly to our local church and ten ministries. We examined all ten very carefully for accountability and for proper moral association and representation. That's 11 unique avenues of compassionate help that we probably would not be able to fund were our taxes higher than they are now. And we hope to give away more as we get raises, tax cuts, or any combination thereof.

The Time Has Come

There is little doubt in my mind that, until we reform the tax code, we will continue to miss opportunities to do amazing acts of compassion. More importantly, we will continue years of discrimination and willfully oppressing the impoverished.

Some people will argue that we can leave this matter for future generations to squabble over. MuscleHeads take a different approach, however.

Because justice for all is fundamentally important to us, we believe that equality and justice should drive us to seek improvements as soon as we possibly can. We believe that every second that passes without taking any action only serves to tarnish the greatness of what could be. We cannot allow passive complacency to lull us to inaction.

That is why we should contact our congressional representatives and senators and press them on the need to change the tax code. But be reminded that these government officials are not always of a mindset to listen. Which is why MuscleHeads must speak in large numbers. The phone number my listeners have become all too familiar with is the magic access code to the nation's capitol—202-334-3121. Using that number, you can request any congressional or senatorial office. Every one of them takes a running poll of what the people are saying to them. Make sure they hear you! Express yourself graciously but firmly.

Perhaps you don't have time to make a phone call, and you find communicating by e-mail much easier. With that in mind, Salem Media, my parent broadcast company, has acquired one of the most exciting political activism Web sites ever to be created, at www.townhall.com. From the main pages you can e-mail any member of Congress. Log on and sound off. Again, remember, your elected officials monitor and tally the data coming in.

And while you're at it, read my blog www.muscleheadrevolu tion.com. I write there daily, and almost always I give instructions on what action you can take if you wish to make a difference as it relates to a specific issue.

You can also participate in the campaign efforts of a candidate who champions true economic equality for all. Campaign work, manning phone banks, and stuffing envelopes all make a difference.

Press your elected officials today! To not do so will leave us in the annals of history with a sad footnote that even we, America, the greatest experiment ever in human government, didn't care enough to do what we knew to be the right thing.

You can be certain you will face tough opposition in the battle to implement a flat tax. You will be demonized; just expect it. But don't be thrown off by it. Stand your ground, proclaim the merits of tax reform, and do what you can to win more minds over to this particular battlefront in the MuscleHead Revolution.

10

The Brazen Tower
of Babel

So where does all this leave us?

All through this book we've identified the source of the faulty thinking that threatens to destroy our society. The people who hold to this kind of thinking comprise the Diabolical Dagger Society. And though on the surface the various members of this society may work more or less independently of one another, they share pretty much the same agenda. We've learned about the ways they undermine commonsense thinking and we've discovered some tactics we MuscleHeads can use to counter their destructive influence. So where does that leave us?

I'm afraid the answer is one we don't want to hear, but we have to be honest with ourselves. The forces of our opponents continue to grow. They are aligning more and more against us. We hear this every night on the television news and see this every day in the headlines. In fact, the brazenness with which the other side acts frequently leaves us feeling helpless. Our souls are agitated. Our hearts know something is amiss. We wish this were a cup that could pass from us. We perhaps have been tempted to hide our head in the sand, hoping that the problem will somehow go away without our intervention, but it won't.

Where do these people get their boldness? What gives them the idea they can act with such arrogance? Why do so many liberals feel so entitled to twist truth and turn it into whatever suits them or to fail to tell both sides of the story?

Historically speaking, the scenario that's facing us is not new. It's happened before. In fact, it happened near the beginning of time.

In Genesis chapter 11 we read about a society very similar to the one in which we live now. Sure, the culture and technology of that day were much more primitive, but the arrogance the people exhibited was very much like that which we see today.

This arrogance escalated to the point where the people decided to build the Tower of Babel. They had grown cocky—like many of the liberals of today—and moved forward with an agenda that appeared quite spectacular, but led to an even more spectacular downfall.

The Bible doesn't say much about the people's motives for building this tower. We're told plainly that the people wanted to make a name for themselves, which makes it evident that pride was involved. It's also safe to speculate that because their goal was to reach the heavens, they may very well have been challenging God in some way. Because of their pride we can be certain these people had a high view of themselves, and because of their attempt to enter the heavens, we can guess they also had a low view of God.

That the people were acting out of rebellion and disobedience is very clear because of the way God reacted to their plan. The judgment He brought upon them was severe and permanent. They brazenly refused to honor God and give Him His rightful place in their lives. They were set on making a name for themselves and challenged God's authority.

And they did this at their own peril.

We see this all over again with many of today's liberals. As we saw earlier in the chapter "It's God, Stupid!" these modern-day counterparts are also brazen in their rebellion against scriptural principles and commonsense thinking. Their agendas reveal a high view of themselves and a low view of God. Their credo is "If it feels good, do it," not "What does God think?" They care about what's expedient, not God's standards. They have usurped God's rightful place in society and life.

And like the people at the Tower of Babel, they do so at their own peril.

Back in the summer of 2005 I started keeping a new file of stories in preparation for my radio show. We keep a lot of different files to help us with show prep, but this one was different. The one common thread that ran through all the stories was the brazenness exhibited by the subjects in the stories.

As I surveyed the contents of this file, a harsh realization settled in upon me. There are many people today who are eager to be the most degrading agents they can possibly be in our culture. Those who make up this crowd are the kind who would wear the popular T-shirt that reads, on the front, "Going to hell as fast as I can…" and on the back, "…and damn proud of it."

It's these people who are taking brazenness to a whole new level. And they could care less what anyone else says or thinks. Or even what God thinks.

I believe there are significant ways in which this utter and willful step toward moral, spiritual, and societal anarchy is coming about, and we need to be wary of them. We need to recognize the gains being made in these arenas—and most importantly, we need to step up our response before these gains push society to the point of no return.

In the rest of this chapter I will break down some defining characteristics of this brazenness, and in the next chapter we will talk about putting into action a biblical, commonsense, MuscleHead response to the matter.

Assessing the Battlefield

This is not an attempt to further define the Diabolical Dagger Society, which is the instigator of the agenda we are warring against. Instead, this is an attempt to give a scout's assessment of the battlefield. We need to recognize that our opponents are well past the point of simply orchestrating their war plan from their operational headquarters. They have already been advancing for some time, and are taking more and more ground.

Sometimes the connection to the three main branches of the DDS—the elites of politics, academia, and entertainment—will be plainly visible. Other times it will require some scrutiny to connect the dots. That is, sometimes it's hard to make the connection between what is being played out on the battlefield and the masterminds who sit in the lofty ivory towers of the Diabolical Dagger Society.

Worse yet is the fact they are counting on the silence and inaction of those who could put a stop to their destructive actions.

You may be surprised to know that, in many ways, the culprit who has allowed the enemy to make so much progress is ourselves. Some of us have fallen asleep at the wheel, so to speak. Though we are well aware of what's going on, we're passive and silent because we've swallowed the lie that it is not proper for people of faith to speak up and defend the truth and moral values.

So we stay silent…and end up giving away important ground. Freedom, the right of spiritual expression, healthy relationships, equal justice, and much more are all under attack. Those who oppose us have dug in deeply, and the shelling has been relentless. And the longer we refuse to do the hard work of fighting back, the harder the battle is going to become because our opponents will have become all the more heavily entrenched and fortified.

Before we look at specific examples of brazenness, let's first look at the reigning philosophy of the day, which helps to foster all the more the atrocities taking place around us today.

The Greatest Source of Damage

The problem that is bringing about the greatest damage upon our society may seem a rather innocuous one. In fact, many of us don't even recognize the danger because we've accommodated ourselves to it.

The God-divide is what separates MuscleHeads from many of those who attack commonsense thinking. And relative thinking is the means by which our opponents have advanced their cause. Relativism says, "There are no absolutes when it comes to what's right and wrong. What's wrong for you might be right for me. It's all a matter of perspective. We're all entitled to our own opinion."

But if you push relativism far enough, you can see it's inherently illogical. A thief obviously will think it's okay to steal your car because, after all, relativism says rightness is merely a matter of perspective.

Relativism empowers people to justify any kind of behavior they want. What if another person's behavior affects us negatively? According to relativism, that's just too bad. In a society where people are free to determine on their own what's right and what's wrong, toes are going to get stepped on. Disagreements are going to flare up. Indeed, relativism is the source of a lot of the conflict we see today between people.

The God who created us, however, intended for us to live by absolutes, which are outlined in the Bible. God's absolutes provide us with clear and consistent guidelines about what is acceptable and what isn't. With absolutes, everyone knows where the boundaries are and what the rules are. With relativism, we're left with a purely arbitrary and philosophical free-for-all. And people are very good at convincing themselves that they are "doing the right thing" even at the expense or harm of others.

If a MuscleHead has the audacity to say that something might not be morally right, the relativists scream, "What's right for you isn't what's right for me." They respond with anger, resentment, and bitterness in the course of what should be a thoughtful and level-headed dialogue about what is good and right. And even when relativists finally realize they have no foundation upon which to stand (because of their illogical reasoning), they continue to scream that they are right even as the ground beneath them collapses.

The Fruit of Relativism

Let's look now at some specific examples of the brazenness that's proliferating in our times.

Lawmakers Who Ignore the Facts

One of the main issues facing American voters in the election of 2004 had to do with the federal judiciary. Each presidential candidate made it clear as to what kind of judges he would pick should he win the election. This issue was one of the major reasons a large percentage of voters went to the polls. In the end, President Bush won. And with the near-immediate retirement of Justice Sandra Day O'Connor, followed by the rather quick passing of Chief Justice Rehnquist, the real battle for the future of the nation's highest court was set in motion.

The John Roberts nomination, which was intended to fill O'Connor's spot but then was changed to fill Rehnquist's spot, was followed by some of the usual and expected rabble-rousing from the liberal members of the Senate. But these opponents did not offer much of a fight because the nomination of Roberts did not threaten to significantly change the balance on the court.

But when Judge Samuel Alito was nominated to fill O'Connor's seat, the liberal members of a judicial committee suddenly became hostile and sank to their lowest depths. The "brazen" factor was highlighted by a number of comments in those hearings. And it all boiled down to this: the Kennedys, Schumers, Durbins, and Leahys of the Senate, all of whom have made their living out of promising the pro-death, pro-abortion special interests groups that they would squash the nomination of anyone who might even remotely be perceived as a threat to the balance of the court in its stance on *Roe v. Wade*.

The millions of dollars given in campaign funds to the majority of the liberal senators who took part in the judiciary nomination hearings have literally allowed them to stay in place through the years to be ready to do combat should conservative nominees ever come to the fore.

And it did not take long for the smear tactics to come forth.

Within the opening minutes of Alito's hearing, the liberals on the committee made it obvious the discussions would have little to do with his abilities as a judge. Rather, they made sure his character and personal integrity came under attack. Some might say that's to be expected, but this was not mere hostility. The verbal sparring descended to outright misrepresentation and lying.

Alito's opponents insisted on trying to paint Alito as racist and sexist on account of vague associations he had with groups from his college days 25 years previous. No concrete evidence was ever brought forward; the accusations were pure hearsay and conjecture.

Especially stunning was Senator Ted Kennedy's public proclamation that Alito had never sided with a "person of color" in a discrimination claim before his court. Between the time Kennedy uttered his ludicrous accusation to the time I went on the air later that afternoon, I was able to turn up no less than five cases in which Alito had sided with victims of discrimination—all of whom were black. The major news networks were also quick to point out Kennedy's mistake. But this didn't faze Kennedy in the least as he continued to repeat, before television cameras, a mantra that had been clearly proven to be false.

Here we had a hardened politician lie to the cameras repeatedly and never even flinch when his bluffs were called. And the American public witnessed firsthand a brazenness without a conscience, a boldness marked by flagrant dishonesty.

The Academy of Brokeback Morality

In 2005 the Hollywood entertainment industry could not understand what was happening. Film receipts as a whole were down. Fewer new releases were matching the income made the previous year. The films that performed the best financially had ratings of G or PG. And among the top five grossing films, only one had an R rating—a comedy titled *Wedding Crashers* which, despite some brief nudity and liberal uses of foul language, ends with a somewhat redemptive message about honesty.

When you compare the list of financially successful films to the list of films that won top honors at the Academy Awards, they're quite different. These two lists give us a small idea of the divide between the entertainment industry and where we MuscleHeads live. Did I say divide? Make that a gorge.

For example, the industry lavished praises upon a film in which a man sought to become a woman through a sex-change operation. Another highly praised film was about two "cowboys" who were married but became attracted to one another and engaged in homosexual activities. In other words, what Hollywood thinks is good and what the average moviegoer will spend the most money on are universes apart.

And this isn't just a recent phenomenon. This gorge has been growing for years. While moviegoers can vote with their pocketbooks and send a message to Hollywood about what they really want, that doesn't diminish the film world's enthusiasm for continuing to produce movies that assault common sense and moral values. Over the decades, Hollywood has managed to slowly but surely lower the bar, and though the movie-going public has by and large expressed reluctance along the way, eventually the outcries have faded away and those things that are immoral and indecent have become more and more the norm.

That which was formerly scandalous has become routine. One by one, the barriers have been knocked down by Hollywood. And look where it's gotten us.

Live Lesbian Porn from Times Square

Yet another example of the assault on our sensibilities took place recently in the middle of Times Square in New York City—one of the most popular tourist destinations in America.

On Valentine's Day 2006, PETA (People for the Ethical Treatment of Animals) waged a demonstration quite different from what anyone might expect of an animal rights organization. PETA hired two attractive female models, clothed them in red silk stockings and matching lingerie, and asked them to literally make out with each other on a large bed—in full view of the public. With the women was a sign that proclaimed, "Vegetarians make better lovers."

For the better part of a week, every person who passed by—including young children—was exposed to this aggressive, indecent, and pornographic display of sexual behavior. Also amazing was that the New York City police did nothing about the demonstration.

This risqué exhibit caused traffic jams as men in the area rushed to snap the salacious scene on their cameras and cell phones. Normally such "entertainment" is available only within the dark confines of a bar. But this took place in the middle of the nation's busiest intersection, and no one took a stand for moral decency—even if just for the sake of the many innocent children who passed by.

MuscleHeads spent the better part of the next several days giving the NYPD and the city mayor's office an earful. Our hope is that such flagrant and public disregard for that which is morally and socially sensible will never be allowed again.

But why should we only be *hopeful* when we should have the right to be *confident?* Why should we have to live in fear that it could happen again? And why should we fear for our children's safety and innocence?

Sex in the School Hallways

It wasn't long ago that parents could more or less count on the public schools in our nation to not only teach the basics and educate their children, but also to protect them from harmful influences in the culture—at least between the hours of 8:00 AM to 4:00 PM Monday through Friday.

Apparently that's no longer the case.

In the February edition of *New York* magazine was a cover story that defied all sensibilities. The scariest part of the story is that it was 100 percent true. It was written as a "several days in the life" of three students who attend one of the New York metro's most well-respected and prestigious college-prep high schools—Stuyvesant High School.

Over the course of some 20 pages, writer Alex Morris detailed graphic sexuality—on the school premises—in ways that almost defy labels.

> Alair is headed for the section of the second-floor hallway where her friends gather every day during their free tenth period for the "cuddle puddle," as she calls it. There are girls petting girls and girls petting guys and guys petting guys. She dives into the undulating heap of backpacks and blue jeans and emerges between her two best friends, Jane and Elle, whose names have been changed at their request. They are all 16, juniors at Stuyvesant. Alair slips into Jane's lap, and Elle reclines next to them, watching, cat-eyed. All three have hooked up with each other. All three have hooked up with boys—sometimes the same boys. But it's not that they're gay or bisexual, not exactly. Not always....
>
> Since the school day is winding down, things in the hallway are starting to get rowdy. Jane disappears for a while and comes back carrying a pint-size girl over her shoulder. "Now I take her off and we have gay sex!" she says gleefully, as she parades back and forth in front of the cuddle puddle. "And it's awesome!" The hijacked girl hangs limply, a smile creeping to her lips. Ilia has stuffed papers up the front of his shirt and prances around on tiptoe, batting his eyes and sticking out his chest. Elle is watching, enthralled, as two boys lock lips across the hall. "Oh, my," she murmurs. "Homoerotica. There's nothing more exciting than watching two men make out." And everyone is talking to another girl in the puddle who just "came out," meaning she announced that she's now open to sexual overtures from both boys and girls, which makes her a minor celebrity, for a little while.[36]

Those two paragraphs barely scratch the surface...

Ten years ago in the halls of Stuyvesant you might have found a few Goth girls kissing Goth girls, kids on the fringes defiantly bucking the system. Now you find a group of vaguely progressive but generally mainstream kids for whom same-sex intimacy is standard operating procedure. "It's not like, *Oh; I'm going to hit on her now.* It's just kind of like, you come up to a friend, you grab their a--," Alair explains. "It's just, like, our way of saying hello." These teenagers don't feel as though their sexuality has to define them, or that they have to define it, which has led some psychologists and child-development specialists to label them the "post-gay" generation. But kids like Alair and her friends are in the process of working up their own language to describe their behavior. Along with gay, straight, and bisexual, they'll drop in new words, some of which they've coined themselves: polysexual, ambisexual, pansexual, pansensual, polyfide, bi-curious, bi-queer, fluid, metroflexible, heteroflexible, heterosexual with lesbian tendencies—or, as Alair puts it, "just sexual." The terms are designed less to achieve specificity than to leave all options open.

To some it may sound like a sexual Utopia, where labels have been banned and traditional gender roles surpassed, but it's a complicated place to be. Anyone who has ever been a girl in high school knows the vicissitudes of female friendships. Add to that a sexual component and, well, things get interesting. Take Alair and her friend Jane, for example. "We've been dancing around each other for, like, three years now," says Alair. "I'd hop into bed with her in a second." Jane is tall and curvy with green eyes and faint dimples. She thinks Alair is "amazing," but she's already had a female friendship ruined when it turned into a romantic relationship, so she's reluctant to let it happen again. Still, they pet each other in the hall, flirt, kiss, but that's it, so far. "Alair," Jane explains, "is literally in love with everyone and in love with no one."[37]

The teens profiled in the article go on to commit to hooking up with each other sexually at least one more time each before graduation, which was later that spring. One of them agreed to be the surrogate mother for another girl's baby. And a bisexual boy agreed to be roommates with the bisexual Alair.

The article went on to detail the sadness that these kids felt. The permanent disconnection is highlighted toward the end of the story when late in the evening the three hook up with another group of kids in a private bedroom and Alair's crush, Jane, ends up having sex with another girl—supposedly breaking Alair's heart. The reporter seemed to indicate that by the next day, however, Alair was already over it and back at life.

The day I came across this article our radio broadcast devoted three full hours to the topic of how brazen and hardened our culture has made our children in matters of personal behavior, and more specifically, sexual behavior. Those three hours were truly heartbreaking as I took call after call from teachers, parents, and students who all said the same thing: "It's worse than you can imagine."

Keep in mind that the teens mentioned in the story were not problem children. They were all Ivy-League bound. They all had high grade-point averages, and in order to even get into Stuyvesant High School they had to have strong recommendations from others.

Of course, upon reading the story, I wondered why the school was not stopping the "cuddle puddle" activities taking place on the school premises. Stuyvesant's administrators at first refused to come on my show or even speak to me. It appears the kids had threatened with lawsuits if they were not allowed to congregate because the activities they engaged in were, from a technical standpoint, legal.

For some weeks following that broadcast, callers continued to ask for more information because they wanted to hold Stuyvesant's feet to the fire. That so many concerned individuals expressed their outrage and disappointment is good. But the fact is, this kind of behavior has not been stopped and is spreading. The assault on morality and public decency continues, and those who are most able to bring an end to it are using the "inability to do anything about it" excuse.

Because of the relative thinking that plagues our society, we can be sure the problem will get worse. We're told if that's what these teens want to do, then we should leave them alone. We're told we shouldn't "impose" our moral values on others.

And in the face of no resistance, the brazen people who are helping to build the modern-day Tower of Babel in our presence will only become bolder.

Fighting Back: There's Strength in Numbers

What is to be done?

In the greatest war of all, brave men from the Allied forces prepared for an invasion on the northern beaches of France. The enemy had well-entrenched positions and superior firepower. General Dwight D. Eisenhower, the supreme Allied commander, knew that there was but one way of taking those shoreheads in order to help the Allied forces know victory against the Nazis in World War II.

The answer was sheer numbers.

It was in numbers of men who would not return home—numbers of men who would drop from the sky or push their way through seawater and climb sand cliffs and do so while taking enemy fire the entire time.

There simply was no other option. And today, we find ourselves in the same dilemma. We have no other option. The war is on. Our enemy sits well entrenched, daring us to take their fire. They are shooting at our homes, families, places of worship, even our own sense of self. And all the while, they are attempting to neutralize the God who made us.

The question now becomes this: Even if we pay a high price as we fight back, isn't the cost of victory quite small compared to the cost of doing nothing? Isn't the value of preserving society and seeing our children whole and healthy worth fighting for with every ounce of strength we have?

I say yes, it's worth it. And there's strength in numbers. How can we make it happen? Read onward...

11

"Crush or Be Crushed!"

As we come to this concluding chapter in *MuscleHead Revolution*, one very important point needs to be made: The time for action is now. To delay even a little bit will only help accelerate our demise.

There's no middle ground in this battle. It's either fight or die. Crush or be crushed.

If that sounds harsh, it's intended to. The Diabolical Dagger Society has set its agenda and is gaining ground at astonishing speed. For MuscleHeads to wait and hope for the best won't do any good. It is time for us MuscleHeads—those of us who use the "sense that is no longer common"—to step up and combat the liberal lunacy that is destroying our society. I know I've been repeating this call to action throughout the book, but given the grave danger we're in, I don't believe it's possible to repeat this call too often.

Consuming Our Children

I'd like to share two more stories that reveal, very painfully, what is taking place in our midst. These stories also reveal the high price of inaction—a price we could very well end up paying if we remain passive on the sidelines. In these particular cases, the price of inaction turned out to be fatal.

During the winter of 2005–06 a story that first broke in the New York media ended up gaining national attention because it was so tragic. A little child who was known for being temperamental was found brutally killed at the hands of her abusive stepfather. Little Nixmary Brown had been chained to a radiator, thrown into a tub of ice-cold water, and repeatedly beaten. Nixmary's mother was also charged in the crimes even though she herself never participated in the abuse.

What did Nixmary do to get such treatment? According to Nixmary's mother, the girl would throw her dinner down the toilet, steal her baby sibling's formula from the refrigerator, and punch and kick her siblings. Generally speaking, Nixmary was a rebellious child who met her demise at the hands of an abusive and severely out-of-control stepfather. And Nixmary's mother felt so intimidated by her husband's temper that she even feared for her own life.

I know it's Monday-morning quarterbacking on my part to raise this question now, but here goes: If in fact Nixmary's mother loved her the way a mother ought to love her daughter, wouldn't she have literally thrown herself between her daughter and husband in order to save her daughter's life?

As it turned out, Nixmary ended up dead because of action on her stepfather's part, and inaction on her mother's.

Again, the story received a lot of attention. Big headlines ran for days all over the media. Meanwhile, half a nation away, little was said about a young man named Dylan.

Dylan Walborn was a four-year-old special-needs child whose life was taken right around the same time as Nixmary's. But sadly, only one paper took the time to print a story about what happened. *Denver Post* reporter Kevin Simpson was given unparalleled access to write a lengthy piece that ran in excess of several thousand words.[38]

Both deaths were tragic, but little Dylan's death was definitely more outrageous because of the manner in which it was carried out and the number of people who had a part. Or, to be more precise, the number of people who didn't do anything to intervene and help Dylan.

Kevin Simpson's account began with some background details about how Dylan's unmarried parents came to the decision to starve him to death. Put simply, they believed it was what he would want. They argued that Dylan suffered a great deal. He had seizures (sometimes as many as four times a day), his body would shiver, he had been born with severe cerebral palsy, he was blind, and he could communicate only nominally. Despite all Dylan's challenges, and the fact that his doctors all said he wouldn't make it to his first birthday, he was well on his way to his fifth when his parents came to the conclusion that he wanted to be starved.

I'll be forthright here: According to the account told in the *Denver Post,* life was hard for Dylan's parents—particularly for his mother, who did the majority of the daily care. This, however, does not justify their choice. The two had decided to marry shortly after she discovered she was pregnant, but due to conflict, they canceled the engagement and never married. Dylan's dad lived less than 200 yards from him and his mother.

The two parents arrived at their decisions to starve Dylan at separate times. His father was the last of the two to inquire about this "solution." He did so after viewing an episode of the television medical drama *House.* While arriving at such a decision is tragic enough, it's what happened afterward that brings us to the most disturbing elements of the story.

According to the reporter, Dylan's parents invited Pastor Buddy Conn from a regional church to come "pray with them" about the option they were investigating. The reporter's account indicates that Pastor Buddy did not "presume to know what to do" in their situation, but lamely expressed "confidence" that God would show them the answer later that day.

That afternoon they all made their way to a hospital and met with Dylan's primary care providers, nurses, and two members of the hospital ethics committee. During this meeting, the hospital decided it would support the starvation of Dylan.

As the rest of the 22-page story unfolds, we read that Dylan's parents set a date for his last feeding, and then planned a "party" for the day before so that Dylan's grandparents, friends, family, and others could "celebrate" Dylan's life. (Even as I type these words the hair is beginning to stand on the back of my neck.)

The reporter made it clear that for the first 18 days or so of Dylan's starvation, no one criticized the parents for their decision. After Dylan's weight dropped from 48 pounds to less than 32, Dylan's mother stopped weighing him. Around this time, Dylan's grandmother was unable to keep her peace any longer. She confronted Dylan's mother, only to be met with scorn and ridicule.

I cried as I read the reporter's description of what happened to Dylan as his life slowly ebbed away. He described Dylan's contorted, starved body, saying that at one point, the core of Dylan's torso was overheated and feverish to the touch, while Dylan's fingers, toes, hands, and feet were literally cold as ice.

Dylan lived for 29 days without food. This was a little more than a full week longer than Terri Schiavo managed to survive when she was starved to death. The article ends with details about Dylan's funeral and some thoughts that Dylan's grandfather expressed about Dylan's dad. The story was sympathetic to Dylan's parents, yet also revealed the very real struggle of conscience that waged within them. Yet we must face the fact this was nothing less than the legalized murder of a five-year-old boy.

That the two stories took place close to the same time struck me. I also couldn't help but feel overwhelmed that both children were betrayed.

The little girl's mother could have done something to save her but didn't. And in the boy's case, betrayal abounded. His parents should have loved and cared for him even in the midst of the pain and discomfort of their own lives. Pastor Buddy Conn should have given the parents proper spiritual guidance and stated that no innocent human life should be taken. The doctors who were charged with Dylan's care should have fought for his right to live. The hospital ethics committee should never have considered it ethically appropriate to starve a five-year-old child to death. And law enforcement authorities should have stepped in when they realized other authorities had missed the mark.

Yet every one of these people had been influenced by modern society's nonsensical maxims that "absolutes are irrelevant" and "if it feels right, do it." In Dylan's case, the right-to-die community had been laying the groundwork for years and had achieved a major milestone when Terri Schiavo was allowed to die. With this foundation in place, all that was necessary was for Dylan's parents to buy into the lie. And tragically, only Dylan's grandmother criticized them along the way. No one else did anything to intervene—not even hospital staff.

The end result was that an innocent boy, who in all honesty probably would not have lived much longer given his condition, died a torturous, painful, unnatural death. He did not have life support removed; he was literally starved. And a number of people who could have helped prevent his premature death did nothing but encourage it.

What if Pastor Buddy, instead of "being afraid to pass judgment," had instead pointed the couple to the fundamental, divine truth that life is precious? What if Dylan's parents had decided to live not by impulse and sleep together, but rather by restraint? We'll never know, but it's possible the determination to honor God's principle to abstain from sex until after marriage would have led to a subsequent determination to be strong and persevere through all Dylan's troubles. What if the hospital ethics committee had flat-out rejected the couple's proposition and said, "No, it is not ethical to starve a child simply because you want to get on with your life. This child *is* your life. How can we help you make the most of it?"

In so many ways, moral clarity was desperately needed. But because of its absence (thanks to the increasing influence of those who undermine commonsense thinking and moral values), an innocent child died before his time.

Caesar Equals We the People

Many people of faith—and this may include you—feel that they simply do not have enough clout or knowledge to speak out and make a difference in the war that rages around us. And there are other people of faith who prefer to remain passive and say, "Kevin, all you can do is pray and let God decide what He will do in the situation." What's scary about that approach is it's the same one Pastor Buddy took when he talked with Dylan's parents. And Dylan's parents ended up doing "whatever felt right" to them. There's a reason God offers us moral guidance and asks us to adhere to it. For us to not do anything is to ignore God's guidelines on how we're to live.

But what if we just don't want to get involved in all the messes that abound in this world?

For Christians, the answer is simple. We are not given an option. There is a well-known story in the New Testament that serves well as an illustration of how we should respond to what's happening around us today.

In Matthew 22:15-22, Jesus' critics tried to trap Him into saying words that would get Him in trouble. They asked Him, "Is it right to pay taxes to Caesar or not?" If Jesus said yes, that would make Him unpopular with the Jewish people, who resented the Roman government's control over their nation. If Jesus said no, He would be accused of tyranny against the Roman government.

How did Jesus reply? "You hypocrites, why are you trying to trap me? Show me the coin used for paying the tax." When His questioners brought forth a coin, Jesus then asked, "Whose portrait is this? And whose inscription?" When his critics said, "Caesar's," Jesus then said, "Give to Caesar what is Caesar's, and to God what is God's."

In other words, we are to honor both God and civil government. Jesus instructed His questioners to fulfill their obligation and to participate in paying the taxes they owed. They were to obey human law so long as it did not violate God's law.

As Christians, we are to do our part when it comes to civil government. And that includes more than just paying taxes. What's more, because we're a democratic society, a government of "we the people," we are, in a sense, Caesar. We live under a government that is by the people and for the people. We're extraordinarily blessed to be living in this land, and we are obligated to participate in the governing process.

As MuscleHeads, we can impact the moral shape of our society.

But how do we start? Let me give you one quick but powerful example.

MuscleHead Moxie

Rebecca Beach is, at the time of this writing, a freshman student at Warren Community College in New Jersey. She arrived with wide-eyed ideals, and she was determined to make a difference.[39]

Her first move was to set up a campus club associated with Young America's Foundation. This tremendous organization helps arm today's young people with clear and commonsense thinking so that they can champion conservative principles, specifically in the arena of education and primarily on today's college campuses.

One of Rebecca's first planned events with her campus club was to invite her peers to come and listen to the decorated War on Terror veteran Lieutenant Colonel Scott Rutter. She and her friends made signs and hoped that the event would attract about 30 to 40 students and faculty. In an effort to bolster the attendance numbers, Rebecca quite innocently asked via a mass e-mail to the faculty for the professors to announce the meeting in their classrooms, and invited them to attend as well.

Rebecca heard back from only one professor. John Daly, a part-time instructor who decided to go ballistic on her. Accusing her group (Young America's Foundation) of being fascist and her of being extreme, he threatened to "expose" the group and run them off the campus. Daly, of course, serves as a fine example of what tolerance truly means to the left.

There is little doubt in my mind that Daly intended to scare Rebecca into inaction and silence. Yet Rebecca understood all too well the concept "crush or be crushed." Being the MuscleHead that she is, she decided to fight back.

Rebecca approached school administrators to inquire about the appropriateness of Daly's behavior. She asked the national leadership of Young America's Foundation for guidance on how she should respond. She came on my show and told her story, and we rallied thousands of phone calls to the school's administration. Eventually the story bubbled up to the Fox News Channel and, before he realized what was happening, Daly's little stunt ended up costing him his job.

Rebecca, a freshman student, simply used the tools at her disposal—especially common sense—to outthink her opponent in the matter. She didn't seek Daly's resignation. All she wanted was for her campus club to have the right to assemble and talk about the War on Terror if the attendees so felt inclined. Daly's attempt to stifle her voice and shut down her club was a vociferous attack not on just her but on the future of political debate on that college campus. Rebecca fought back—and though she was one freshman student, she was able to make a difference that benefited her entire campus.

Rebecca's example teaches us some practical ways that we, too, can engage in the fight.

Tactics for Success

1. *Arm yourself with faith and truth.* It is imperative to understand the basics of your faith. It is also important to know the facts related to the issue at hand. So where do you turn? I am of course partial to the broadcast that I slave over every single day to bring the latest issues to the forefront. We are streamed on RadioAOL. And for you non-AOL users, we also offer streaming options at MuscleHeadRevolution.com and WMCA.com. And if you prefer the "listen on demand option," all 15 hours of my daily show are now available in crystal-clear MP3 podcasting. At this time it is a completely free service, and will continue to be as long as I have a say in the matter. The MuscleHead broadcast runs from 2:00 to 5:00 p.m. Eastern Standard Time.

    In addition to listening, I also strongly urge you to check Internet outlets that you can trust for an honest take on the day's news. On page 197 is an appendix that provides a list of Internet sites and blogs that I read regularly, even if only for a few seconds a day. Any half dozen of these will give you a good idea of which news stories should be of concern to you.

    By staying informed, or seeking the right guidance, you will know how to respond to your attackers. And by standing firm on the Rock of Ages, you will have a foundation that cannot be shaken.

2. *Spread the word.* It's not enough to just know the issues and discuss them intelligently. You want to share your knowledge with others so that they, too, can use common sense to overturn liberal thinking. Through the use of e-mail lists, blogs, and other modern technologies, you can easily inform your circle of friends about the important challenges you are dealing with in your corner of the Revolution.

3. *Keep pressing on.* Not everyone will come to appreciate the commonsense perspectives you share. Some people might shrug you off, and others may even reject you outright. At times you will feel like the odds are overwhelming and that you're all alone. Don't let that discourage you. Keep pressing on.

When I first came to New York City, I was told that my broadcast was not appreciated. I was pegged as a token right-winger who would be utterly lost and useless in a liberal city like New York. But in less than one year's time, I found the exact opposite to be true. I was challenging people to use common sense to analyze various social and political problems, and a surprisingly large number of people in New York City have expressed their appreciation for this. For the most part they've been an unheard-of constituency because they had no media figure speaking for them. What's more, we've gotten many calls from people who formerly disliked the broadcast but now support it.

Especially gratifying is the fact we have a metro-area church community that has been strong in numbers (over 8000 churches in metro New York City) but weak in strength—and the broadcast has lit a fire under them to be more bold about using common sense to overturn the status quo in one of America's most liberal cities.

Never Surrender

One of my longtime heroes is Sir Winston Churchill. He became
the prime minister of Great Britain in 1940 and succeeded Neville
Chamberlain, who became controversial in the late 1930s for giving
in to Adolph Hitler's demands instead of standing up to him. Little
did Churchill know when he took this new post, that Great Britain
was about to enter some very dark years. Matters took a turn for the
worse when France, an important ally, fell to Germany. Through
most of the war, life was very difficult and bleak in Great Britain. As
the fighting dragged on, people began to doubt Churchill more and
more. His critics mocked him for his simple, straightforward logic
and plainness of thinking. Germany's persistent bombing raids over
London instilled fear in the British populace. The situation became
so bad people felt certain that Hitler would invade and conquer the
British Isles.

Fortunately, Churchill knew the best way to deal with this
growing fear. Summoning his considerable skills of oratory, he
addressed the Parliament and the world on June 4, 1940 and
proclaimed,

> We shall not flag nor fail. We shall go on to the end. We shall
> fight in France and on the seas and oceans; we shall fight with
> growing confidence and growing strength in the air. We shall
> defend our island whatever the cost may be; we shall fight on
> beaches, landing grounds, in fields, in streets and on the hills.
> We shall never surrender and even if, which I do not for the
> moment believe, this island or a large part of it were subjugated
> and starving, then our empire beyond the seas, armed and
> guarded by the British Fleet, will carry on the struggle until in
> God's good time the New World with all its power and might,
> sets forth to the liberation and rescue of the Old. [40]

Churchill stood strong in the face of overwhelming opposition.
He did not give up; he was determined to persevere. We who

are MuscleHeads can learn from Churchill's example as we work together to rescue and preserve common sense. We need to take a stand for the good of our families, our children, our beliefs, and our future. We cannot allow ourselves to think that the battle is too far gone and that defeat is inevitable. That's how it looked in Great Britain, but because of his determination, Churchill was able to turn the tide in his favor. Likewise, no matter how dismal today's situation looks, we must hold tenaciously to the hope of victory.

We must be willing to charge out of our foxholes instead of merely holding to a defensive posture. We must arm ourselves with the principles that we know to be true and proclaim them without apology. We can no longer afford to sit quietly as our children's minds, hearts, and even bodies are consumed by the moral relativism of our day.

The reason the opposition has gained so much ground in this battle is because we have done little or nothing to stop them. We did not choose this conflict, and therefore we would prefer that others do the fighting. Or, we may even hope that somehow, things will take care of themselves without any intervention on our part. The problem is, because we have chosen to stay out of the conflict, we have unwittingly helped to prolong it.

But no more!

Today we must commit to saying and doing that which is true, just, and good. Like Rebecca Beach, we must find out what tools we have at our disposal. We might not have much clout, but neither did Rebecca Beach. Yet she was able to achieve some very remarkable results.

We can do the same as we defend the principles of the MuscleHead Revolution.

And on the following oath we make our stand!

The Official MuscleHead
"Declaration of Revolution"

Whereas it is commonly recognized that there is now in effect a war that is ravaging our children and the future they will inherit.

Whereas we recognize that the opponent in this conflict has been steadily on the offensive for more than a generation and originates from within our very borders.

Whereas we recognize that the opponent in this conflict associates with the most diabolical of persons and philosophies known to man. Whereas we recognize that the opponent in this matter uses dagger-like weapons of stealth and deception. Whereas it is also acknowledged this enemy resides in the elite places within society and looks upon mainstream society with disdain.

Whereas we do acknowledge that this war is not a conflict of our choosing nor one of our liking.

Whereas it is also commonly recognized, if not by those who have and can exercise the implementation of common sense to help resolve such conflicts, that those of us who can recognize such conflicts upon our lives and oath do pledge the following:

Be it resolved that we not only recognize the existence of our Creator but freely and with all soberness of mind put our faith in His truth.

Be it resolved that because of such a source of strength as our Creator, who is a very Rock on which we can stand and not be shaken, we do recognize that it is imperative for the well-being of our families, children, and selves that we choose to live not by the lowest common impulse as such may often course through our veins. Be it instead that we shall cause a revival in which restraint and forethought will once again be exercised in our lives and time.

Be it resolved that we also seek the sense which is no longer common. Yet we know the hope of its abundance as it stems from the same Creator who created us.

Be it resolved that we deliberately acknowledge and do hereby proclaim that the equality of men and women shall never be in question. Yet we do also adhere to the eternal principle that is self-evident which says that men and women are not the same. Never shall we accept sameness as a fraudulent substitute for true equality. Nor shall we ever diminish the importance of men being men and women being women.

Be it resolved that we do not now, nor shall we in the days of uncertainty that lay in front of us, yield the meanings of language. We shall instead be eternally devoted to the vigilance of meaning, clarity, and integrity of the spoken and written word.

Be it resolved that those who hold to true conservative MuscleHeaded ideas do hereby proclaim that compassion is key, even central to our view of the world and our hope for the future.

Be it resolved that we promise and do by the oath of our namesake pledge for eternity to treat all men with dignity, respect, and all other social graces which affirm their equality in this life, and their importance to God our Creator. Be it also resolved that we will seek to proactively tear down walls of discrimination, prejudice, and injustice for the sake of the good of our brother who stands with us.

Be it resolved that we will fight, pray, and work for a tax and economic system which spreads both its benefits and its burdens as evenly as is possible.

Be it resolved that we recognize and do pledge our resistance to the brazen, crass, and hardened elements of society that seek to destroy us, our faith, and our families.

And be it resolved that we shall stay offensive in these matters for as long as is necessary to effectively conquer the issues at stake before us and win the just and proper equity in matters to come. We recognize that defensive posturing has done little of substance in the past and seek radical reform of this world's social and political environments for the cause of all that is true, just, and good.

Be it resolved that by signing to these resolutions, we shall be linked as brothers in the revolution that is before us, and thus our title shall from now on be called *MuscleHead.*

*(Friend, if you so choose to take these resolutions to heart and to join this MuscleHead Revolution, please send me an e-mail so that we can add your name as an original signatory to this Declaration of Revolution that will be put on display in the MuscleHead Revolution broadcast headquarters. My e-mail address is MuscleHead@wmca.com. Please include **only** your first and last name and the city in which you live.)*

Acknowledgments

So many I need to express tremendous thanks to…

God, my Father and Christ, my Savior—for the sovereignty You exercise in my life and in this world. Knowing You are in control brings sanity to the insane reality that is now upside-down from the way You created it to be. Thank You for Your creation, Your mercy, Your grace, and Your love.

The Lovely Bride—in so many ways you have helped this man who found himself in the most upside-down of worlds and through your gentleness and love helped coax him right-side up again. I don't remember what life was like before you. And I am grateful for every minute you spend with me in this journey. Thank you for your endless support and encouragement. You are a wellspring of joy for a tired old soul like me.

My son—you may never have the capacity to even read these words, but what the world will read is that your father loves you, prays for you, and longs for you to have the discernment to be the MuscleHead God made you to be. Even in your simple experiences you teach me things every day. I love you!

To Dr. Ray Pritchard—many thanks...for your godly wisdom, practical insight, and sometimes tough words. Thanks especially for letting me in at 3 AM, to gripe at God, to weep in my moment of loss with me, and to point me to Psalm 115:3. Thanks also for kicking me back out the door and pushing me to get on with life. I'm tryin', Pastor Ray, I'm tryin'...

Many thanks also to Steve Miller at Harvest House Publishers. His refinement of my ideas and his sharpening of my pen is evident all over this manuscript.

To Bob Hawkins and the entire Harvest House family—thanks for taking a chance on me.

To Gary Villapiano—for being my MuscleHead partner, and for standing tall in making as much trouble as we can possibly get into...

To Ed Atsinger, Joe Davis, Dave Armstrong, and Salem Media— thanks for giving my voiced ideas the power to soar.

And last but by no means least the listeners of WMCA 570/970 in New York, WYLL AM 1160 and WMBI AM and FM in Chicago, KCBI in Dallas, Salem Media, Moody Broadcasting, and Criswell Radio Networks—many of you, at significant points in time, picked up the phone, stated an opinion, gave a word of criticism, or burst forth with a word of encouragement that I would not have gotten any other way. It is you I serve, and it is you I ask to march with us...in the *MuscleHead Revolution!*

Appendix
Additional Daily Information Source

General News

The Drudge Report—http://drudgereport.com

Fox News—http://foxnews.com

CNN—http://cnn.com

WorldNetDaily—http://www.wnd.com

Beyond the News—http://beyondthenews.com

TownHall—http://townhall.com

Washington Times—http://www.washtimes.com

Wall Street Journal—http://online.wsj.com

The Weekly Standard—http://weeklystandard.com

NewsMax—http://newsmax.com

National Review Online—http://www.nationalreview.com

Specialty Voices in the Blogosphere

Instapundit—http://www.instapundit.com

Hugh Hewitt—http://hughhewitt.com

Kevin McCullough—http://muscleheadrevolution.com

Michelle Malkin—http://michellemalkin.com

Red State—http://redstate.org

Real Clear Politics—http://realclearpolitics.com
PowerLine—http://powerlineblog.com
Little Green Footballs—http://www.lgf.com
Captain's Quarters—http://captainsquartersblog.com
The Corner NRO—http://corner.nationalreview.com
Expose the Left—http://exposetheleft.com

Notes

1. Jane Roh, "Supreme Court Bars Commandments from Courthouses," Fox News, June 27, 2005.
2. Larry Celona, Lorena Mongelli, Brigitte Williams, "Little Girl Kills Her 'Sis,'" *New York Post*, May 31, 2005.
3. Bart Jones, "Cops: Mom killed in fight over chore," *New York Newsday*, May 31, 2005.
4. Christine Armario, "Fatal dad-son spat," *New York Newsday*, May 31, 2005.
5. Kate Roberts, "Teen Kills Six on Graduation Day," CBS News, May 31, 2005.
6. Associated Press, "Florida Teens Accused in Homeless Killing," ABC News, May 30, 2005.
7. Dr. Cary Savitch, *The Nutcracker Is Already Dancing* (Ventura, CA: Teague House, 1996).
8. Wikipedia, s.v. "Common sense," http://wikipedia.org.
9. Wikipedia, s.v. "Gloria Steinem."
10. Susan B. Anthony, *The Revolution*, July 8, 1869, p. 4.
11. Mattie Brinkerhoff, *The Revolution*, September 2, 1869, pp. 138-39.
12. Kathleen Barry, *Susan B. Anthony: A Biography of a Singular Feminist* (New York: Ballantine Books, 2000), p. 34.
13. "Move over, Rambo, you're cramping new man's style," Agence France Press, June 8, 2005.
14. Ibid.
15. Ibid.
16. *Report of the Joint Select Committee to Inquire into the Condition of Affairs in the Late Insurrectionary States, vol. 2* (Washington, DC: Government Printing Office, 1872; reprint New York: AMS Press, 1968), p. 220; also vol. 3, pp. 26-27.

17. *Report of the Joint Select Committee to Inquire into the Condition of Affairs in the Late Insurrectionary States, vol. 3* (Washington, DC: Government Printing Office, 1872; reprint New York: AMS Press, 1968), p. 27; also vol. 4, p. 848; vol. 7, p. 1005; vol. 9, p. 899; vol. 11, p. 286.

18. David Barton, Wallbuilders Presentation, July 2005. Presented to the Christian Action Coalition in New York City and followed by a live Muscle-Head Radio broadcast covering the same material.

19. There are serious problems with the attempts to prove that homosexuality is genetic in origin—see Mike Haley, *101 Frequently Asked Questions About Homosexuality* (Eugene, OR: Harvest House Publishers, 2004), pp. 189-99.

20. From a speech given by George W. Bush in Palm Beach, Florida on June 8, 2004.

21. *Report of the Joint Select Committee to Inquire into the Condition of Affairs in the Late Insurrectionary States, vol. 1* (Washington, DC: Government Printing Office, 1872; reprint New York: AMS Press, 1968), pp. 27-34.

22. See Wikipedia, s.v. "Black Reconstruction" at http://en.wikipedia.org/wiki/Reconstruction, 2006, and also Walter Lynwood Fleming, *The Sequel of Appomattox: A Chronicle of the Reunion of the States* (Whitefish, MT: Kessinger Publishing, 2003), pp. 54-64, 80-82.

23. *Report of the Joint Select Committee to Inquire into the Condition of Affairs in the Late Insurrectionary States, vol. 1* (Washington, DC: Government Printing Office, 1872; reprint New York: AMS Press, 1968), p. 28.

24. David Barton, Wallbuilders Presentation, July 2005. Presented to the Christian Action Coalition in New York City and followed by a live MuscleHead Radio broadcast covering the same material.

25. Rep. Richard Cain speech on Civil Rights Bill, February 3, 1875, as cited in *Congressional Record, 43rd Congress, 2nd Session, vol. 3* (Washington, DC: Government Printing Office, 1875), p. 957.

26. Bernard Schwartz, *Statutory History of the United States, Civil Rights, Part 1* (New York: Chelsea House Publishers, 1970), p. 803.

27. The absence of any Democratic call for a ban on lynching is evident in Donald B. Johnson, ed., *National Party Platforms 1840–1976, Supplement 1980* (Champaign-Urbana, IL: University of Illinois Press, 1982).

28. *Congressional Record, 81st-85th Congress, All Sessions* (Washington, DC: United States Government Printing Office, 1950–62).

29. Walter E. Williams, *Civil Rights Today*, August 17, 2005 at Townhall.com (originally credited to Marc Moreno, Cybercast News Service).

30. Ibid.

31. Ibid.

32. Marc Moreno, *GOP Group Tries to Halt Black Voter Loyalty to Dems*, Cybercast News Service, August 15, 2005.

33. *The National Center for Educational Statistics, 2005 Assessment Results, Reading Results: Executive Summary for Grades 4-8, National Results, Reading Re-*

sults for Student Group at Age 4, paragraph 1 (at Grade 8, paragraph 1). As cited by Bishop Harry Jackson on MuscleHead Radio, August 23, 2005. See also Jackson's "Black Contract with America on Moral Values," released February 1, 2005 by the High-Impact Leadership Coalition, as well as his book *High Impact African-American Churches* (Ventura, CA: Gospel Light, 2004).

34. Christopher Dodd speech given on April 1, 2004, as cited on Open World News at www.openworldnews.com.

35. Haley, *101 Frequently Asked Questions About Homosexuality,* pp. 189-99.

36. Alex Morris, "The Cuddle Puddle of Stuyvesant High School," *New York,* February 6, 2006, p. 1. Used with permission.

37. Ibid., p. 2. Used with permission.

38. Kevin Simpson, "Letting Go: Dylan's last days, two parents face an agonizing test of faith and love for their son," *Denver Post,* December 18, 2005.

39. Kevin McCullough, "Prof. to Soldiers: Kill Officers in Iraq," WorldNet-Daily, November 18, 2005.

40. Winston Churchill in a speech before the House of Commons on June 4, 1940, as cited at http://history.hanover.edu/courses/excerpts/111chur.html.